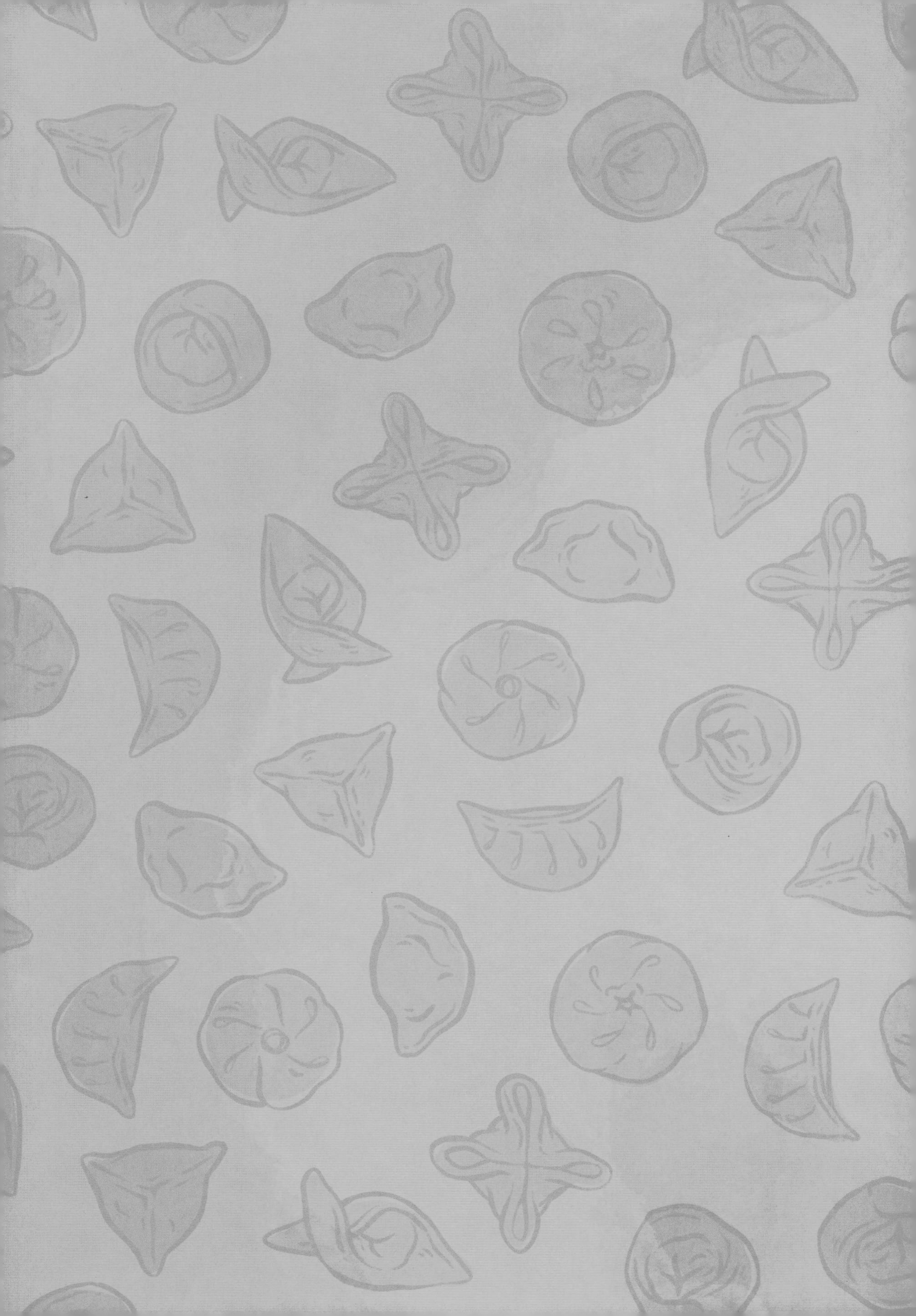

LET'S MAKE DUMPLINGS!

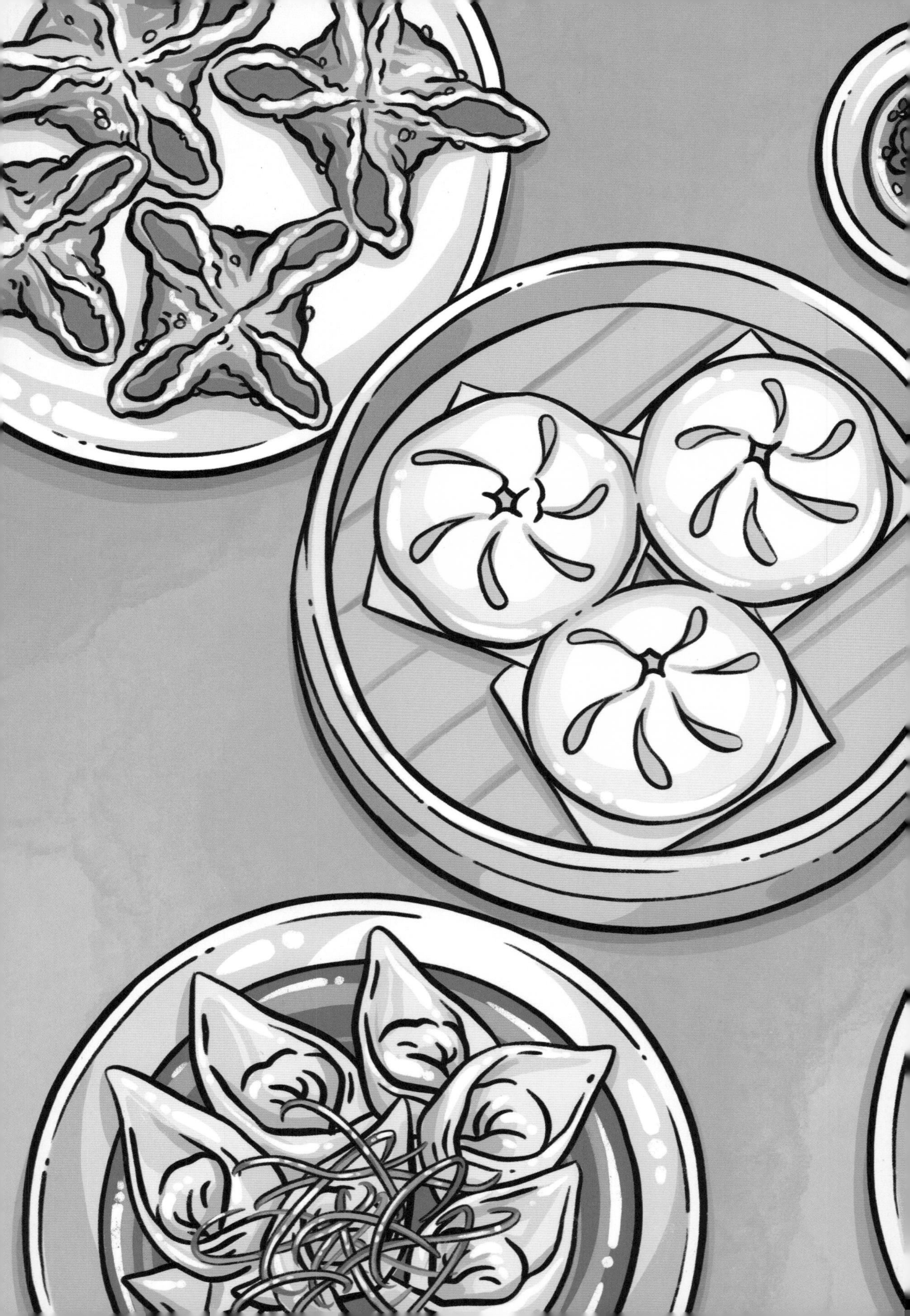

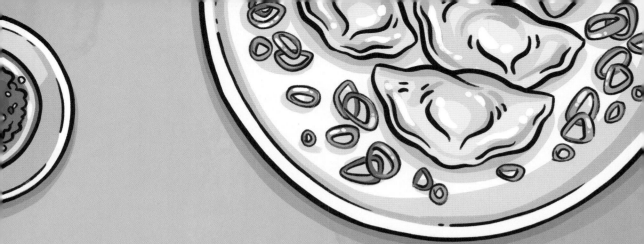

LET'S MAKE DUMPLINGS!

HUGH AMANO   SARAH BECAN

A COMIC BOOK COOKBOOK

TEN SPEED PRESS
CALIFORNIA | NEW YORK

TABLE OF

CONTENTS

INTRODUCTION

WE'RE BACK! I'M HUGH, A CHEF AND WRITER,

AND I'M SARAH, AN ILLUSTRATOR.

YOU MAY HAVE MADE RAMEN WITH US FROM OUR BOOK *LET'S MAKE RAMEN!*

WE'RE LOOKING FORWARD TO EXPLORING ANOTHER DELICACY WITH YOU: DUMPLINGS!

WE'RE FASCINATED BY THE WORLD OF TASTY FILLINGS ENCASED IN CHEWY WRAPPERS

AND COULD SPEND A LIFETIME EXAMINING ALL THE DUMPLINGS THE WORLD HAS TO OFFER.

BUT FOR NOW, LET'S FOCUS ON ONE OF THE LARGEST CATEGORIES OUT THERE: ASIAN DUMPLINGS.

IN THIS BOOK, WE'LL PRESENT SEVERAL RECIPES FOR SAVORY — AND SOME SWEET! — DUMPLINGS

WHILE TOUCHING ON SOME OF THEIR HISTORICAL AND CULTURAL ELEMENTS.

WE'LL TEACH YOU HOW TO MAKE YOUR OWN DUMPLING WRAPPERS

AND HOW STORE-BOUGHT WRAPPERS CAN BE SUBSTITUTED.

YOU'LL LEARN A VARIETY OF FOLDING TECHNIQUES AND COOKING METHODS,

AND WE'LL GUIDE YOU THROUGH SEVERAL SAUCE RECIPES.

WE'LL ALSO INCLUDE WHICH FOLDS, COOKING METHODS, AND SAUCES GO WITH WHICH DUMPLINGS!

WE'LL HELP YOU BUILD A PANTRY FILLED WITH NECESSARY INGREDIENTS AND EQUIPMENT,

ALL WITH THE GOAL OF GETTING YOU READY TO WOW THE WORLD WITH YOUR NEWFOUND DUMPLING SKILLS!

SO LET'S GET WRAPPING AND DIPPING!

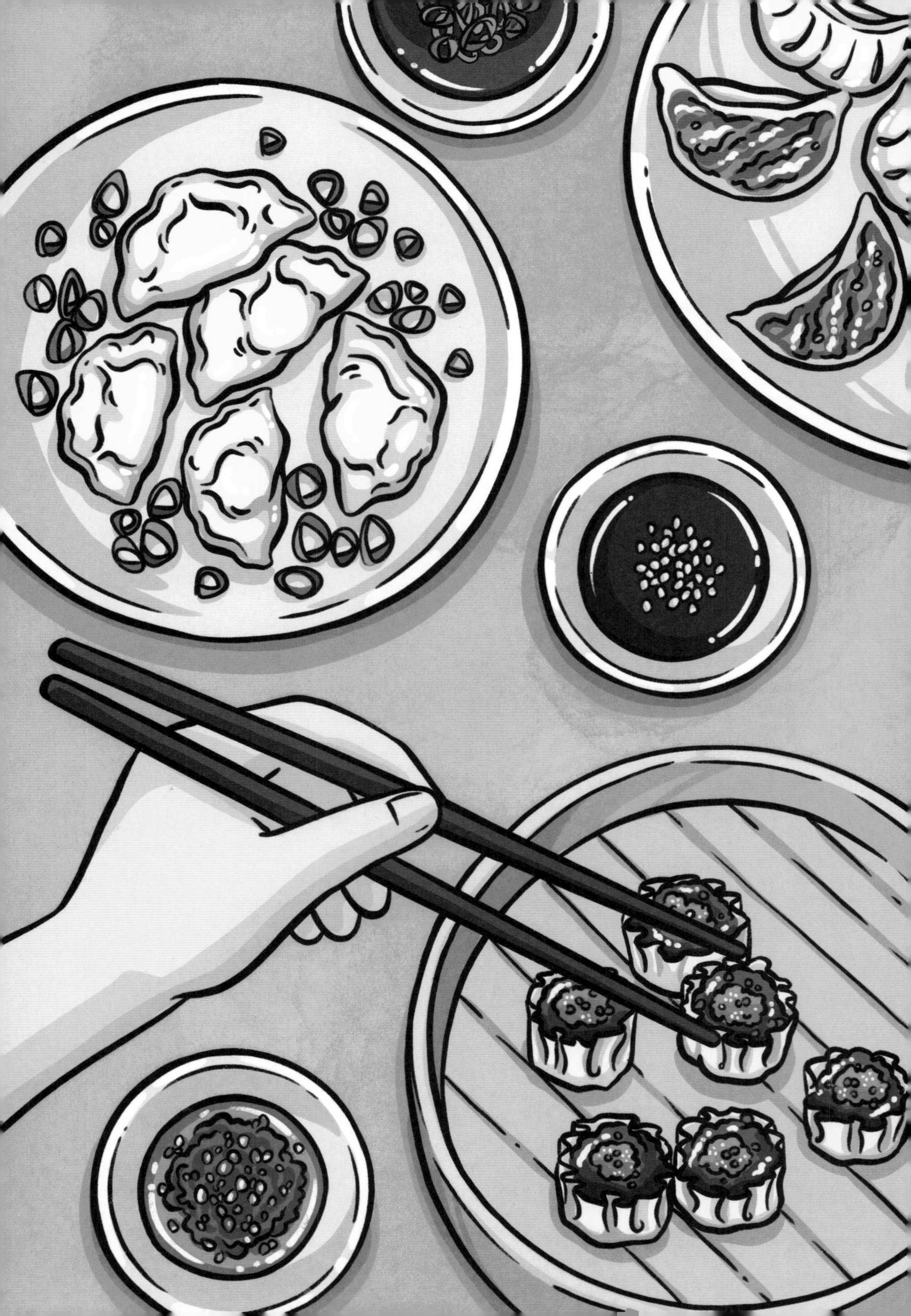

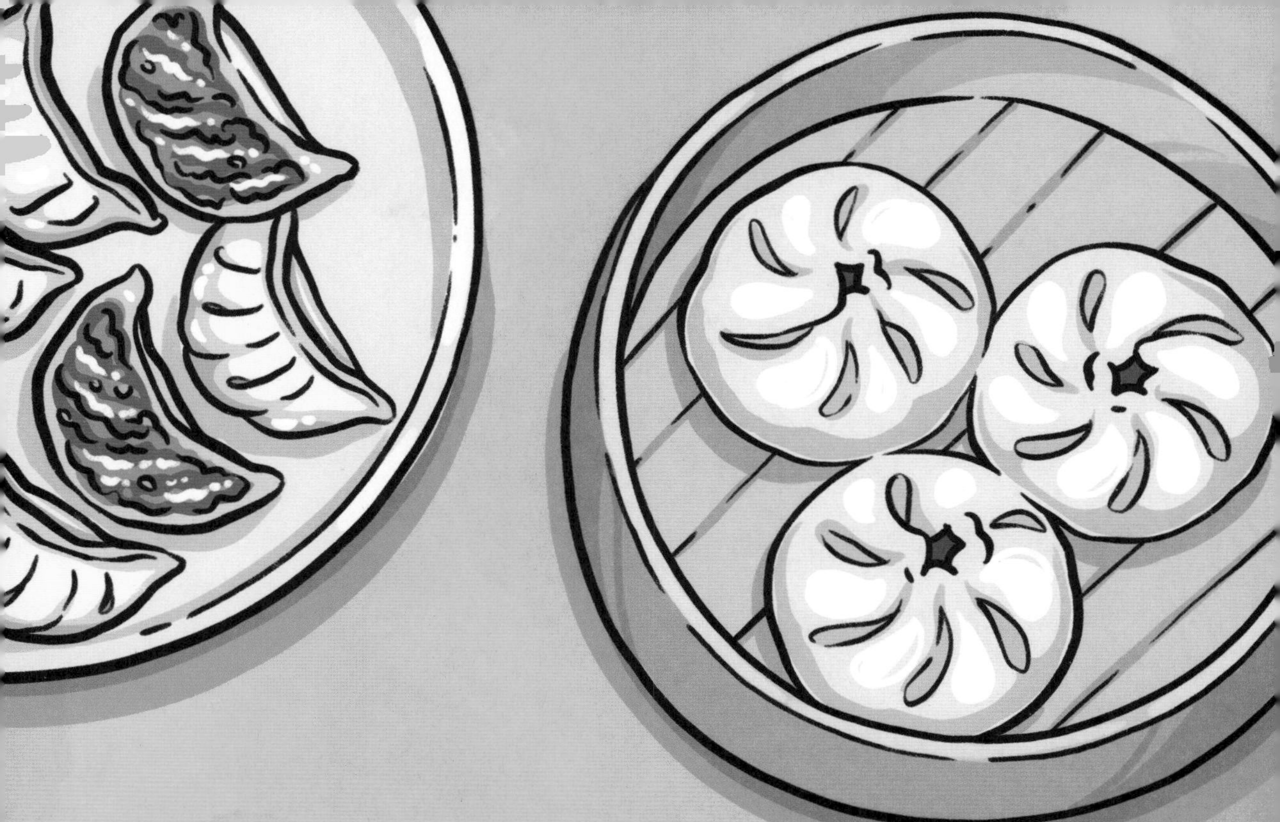

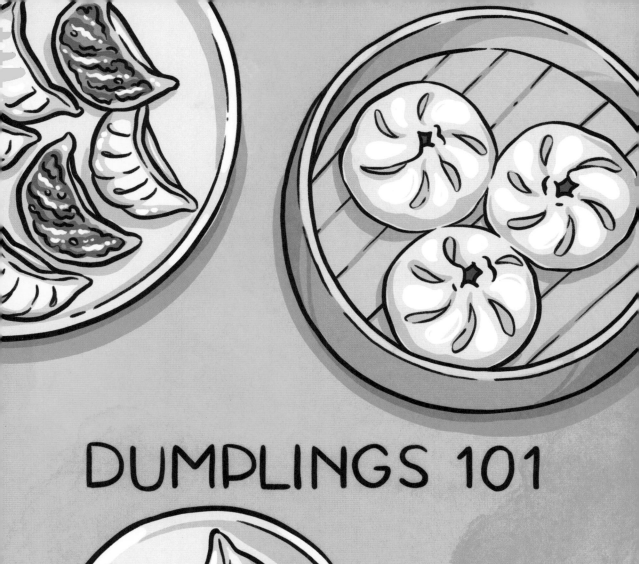

DUMPLINGS 101

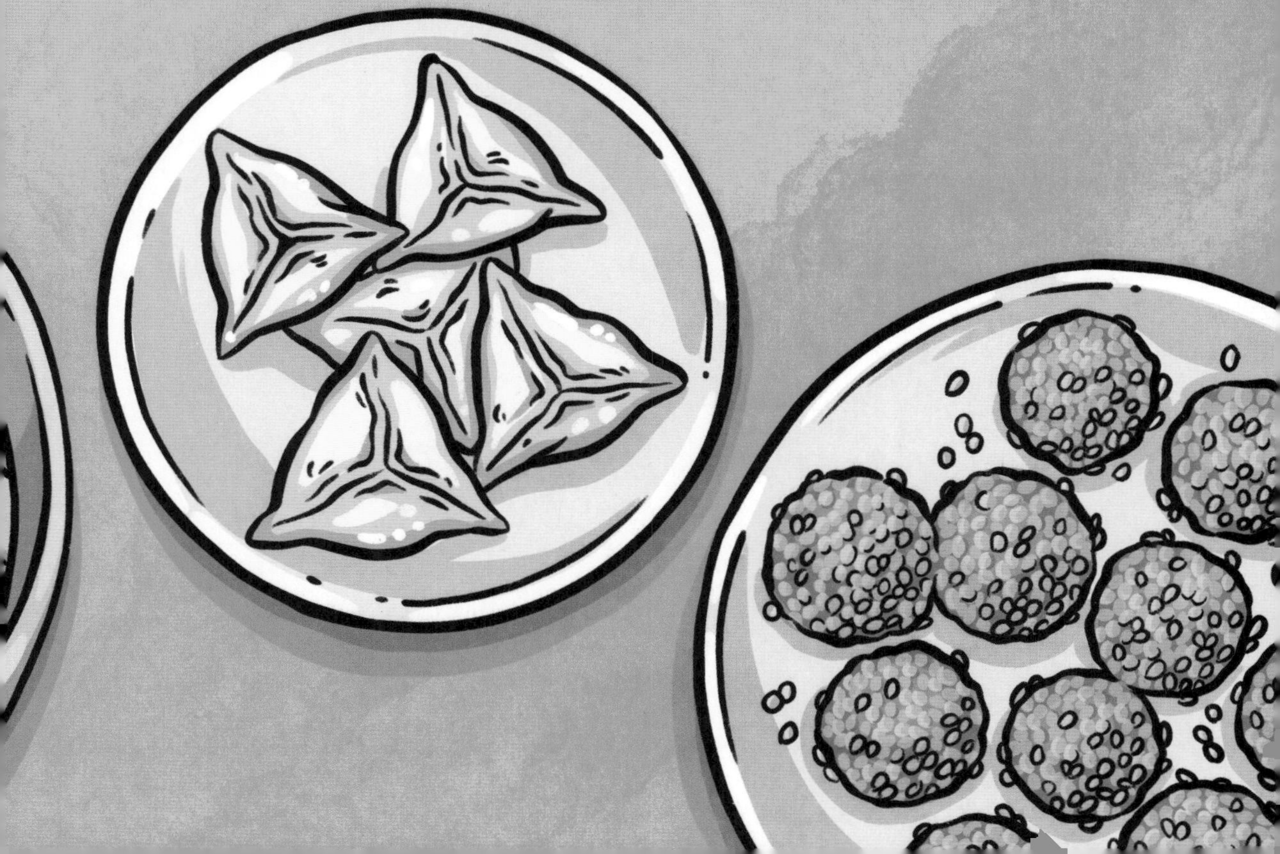

a bit of DUMPLING LORE

WE'D BE HARD-PRESSED TO NAME A CULTURE IN THE WORLD THAT DOESN'T HAVE SOMETHING THAT COULD BE CALLED A DUMPLING:

FROM FILLED PASTAS LIKE ITALIAN TORTELLINI AND POLISH PIEROGI,

TO LESS OBVIOUS TYPES OF DUMPLINGS, LIKE MEXICAN TAMALES AND ARGENTINEAN EMPANADAS,

TO UNFILLED GERMAN SPAETZLE AND CHICKEN AND DUMPLINGS FROM THE U.S.

SINCE WE'RE LOOKING AT FILLED ASIAN DUMPLINGS HERE,

IS THERE ANY WAY TO REALLY KNOW EXACTLY WHERE THEY FIRST ORIGINATED?

AS POPULAR LEGEND TELLS IT, ZHANG ZHONGJING,

AN ELITE CHINESE PHYSICIAN OF THE EASTERN HAN DYNASTY (SPANNING THE FIRST TWO CENTURIES AD),

CAME ACROSS A GROUP OF IMPOVERISHED PEOPLE DURING AN ESPECIALLY BRUTAL WINTER.

THE POOR CONDITIONS THEY WERE ENDURING MANIFESTED AS FROSTBITE ON THEIR EARS.

WANTING TO EASE THEIR SUFFERING, ZHANG STEWED MUTTON,

MIXED IN HERBS TO AID BLOOD FLOW,

AND WRAPPED THE FILLING IN WHEAT DOUGH, FORMING FILLED DUMPLINGS RESEMBLING EARS.

HE BOILED THE DUMPLINGS IN THE MUTTON'S COOKING LIQUID,

AND SERVED THEM — TWO FOR EACH BOWL — IN THE BROTH.

THE HOT BROTH AND FORTIFYING DUMPLINGS CIRCULATED WARMTH THROUGHOUT THE CHILLED PEOPLE

AND FOUGHT OFF THE WINTER'S ILL EFFECTS.

THE HISTORICAL ACCURACY OF THAT TALE IS LOST TO THE AGES, BUT THE FUNDAMENTAL TRUTH PERSEVERES:

FROSTBITE OR NO,

SINKING YOUR TEETH INTO A BUNDLE OF FLAVORFUL, AROMATIC MEAT AND VEGETABLES WRAPPED IN A SOFT DOUGH

TRANSCENDS ANY IMAGINED BORDERS OF CULTURE AND CASTE,

AND IS FULFILLING FOR THE NOURISHED AND NURTURER ALIKE.

IN SHORT, EVERYBODY LOVES A GOOD DUMPLING, SO LET'S MAKE SOME!

DUMPLINGS TO UNITE US ALL!

A WORLD OF

POTSTICKER

MOMO

A NOTE ON THE DUMPLINGS
IN THIS BOOK:

THE DUMPLINGS THAT APPEAR IN
THIS BOOK ARE PART OF A MUCH
LARGER WORLD OF DUMPLINGS
SPANNING ASIA (AND THE ENTIRE
GLOBE FOR THAT MATTER!).

AFTER YOU READ THIS BOOK,
WE ENCOURAGE YOU TO EMBARK
ON YOUR OWN RESEARCH, TRAVEL,
AND EXPLORATION OF ALL THE
WONDERFUL DUMPLINGS THAT
ARE OUT THERE, AND EVEN
PUT YOUR OWN SPIN ON
TRADITIONAL RECIPES.

DUMPLINGS

BUUZ

BAOZI

JIAOZI

MANDU

GYOZA

SHENG JIAN BAOZI

JIAN DUI

CRAB RANGOON

XIAOLONGBAO

WONTON

SHUMAI

NAI HUANG BAOZI

NUM KOM

KAYA BAOZI

SIOPAO

PANTRY

DUMPLINGS DON'T REQUIRE A HUGE AMOUNT OF OBSCURE INGREDIENTS, BUT HERE ARE A FEW ITEMS TO KEEP AROUND THAT WILL MAKE THE PROCESS SIMPLER.

BLACK CHINKIANG VINEGAR

AGED AND FUNKY, CHINESE BLACK CHINKIANG VINEGAR BRINGS A MOLASSES-LIKE, ALMOST BALSAMIC VINEGAR–LIKE QUALITY TO SAUCES AND DUMPLINGS. YOU CAN SUBSTITUTE BALSAMIC VINEGAR IN A PINCH, BUT YOU'LL BE ABLE TO FIND BLACK VINEGAR, OFTEN LABELED CHINKIANG VINEGAR, FOR THE EASTERN CHINESE CITY IT IS FROM, IN ASIAN MARKETS AND ONLINE.

FISH SAUCE

COMMON IN SOUTHEAST ASIA, FISH SAUCE BRINGS A STRONG, SALTY DEPTH OF UMAMI FLAVOR WITHOUT ACTUALLY MAKING ANYTHING "FISHY." IT CAN BE FOUND IN MOST MAJOR GROCERY STORES AND IN ASIAN MARKETS.

GLUTINOUS RICE FLOUR

HIGH IN STARCH AND OFTEN LABELED AS SWEET RICE FLOUR, GLUTINOUS RICE FLOUR IS WIDELY USED IN ASIAN CONFECTIONS. LOOK FOR IT IN ASIAN MARKETS, THE SPECIALTY FLOUR SECTION OF YOUR GROCERY STORE, OR ONLINE. GLUTINOUS RICE FLOUR IS THE MAIN INGREDIENT IN A COUPLE OF RECIPES IN THIS BOOK, SO BE SURE NOT TO SUBSTITUTE ANY OTHER FLOUR FOR IT.

MIRIN

MIRIN IS A SWEETENED JAPANESE RICE WINE USED TO SEASON EVERYTHING FROM SAUCES TO SOUPS TO SUSHI RICE IN JAPANESE COOKING. WE USE IT IN MANY OF OUR DUMPLINGS FOR ITS COMPLEX SWEETNESS AND SUBTLE RICHNESS. MIRIN IS WIDELY AVAILABLE IN MOST GROCERY STORES AND SHOULD BE SOUGHT OUT FOR ITS UNIQUE FLAVOR. IF YOU'RE IN A PINCH, SWEETEN SIX PARTS RICE VINEGAR WITH ONE PART SUGAR FOR A PASSABLE APPROXIMATION.

NEUTRAL OIL

WHEN WE REFER TO "NEUTRAL OIL" IN THIS BOOK, WE SIMPLY MEAN A VEGETABLE OIL WITH UNASSERTIVE AROMA AND FLAVOR, SUCH AS CANOLA OIL, PEANUT OIL, GRAPESEED OIL, OR A BLENDED VEGETABLE OIL. AROMATIC AND FLAVORFUL OILS, SUCH AS UNREFINED COCONUT OIL AND OLIVE OIL, WILL ADD CONFLICTING FLAVORS AND WILL BURN MORE EASILY WHEN USED AS A FRYING MEDIUM.

SHAOXING WINE

THIS RICE WINE FROM EASTERN CHINA IS AGED IN CLAY POTS FOR DRINKING AND COOKING — THINK DISHES SUCH AS "DRUNKEN CHICKEN" AND THE LIKE. BUT IT NEEDN'T BE AS OBVIOUS AS THAT — SHAOXING WINE IS USED IN MARINADES AND SAUCES TO BRING AN AGED, OXIDIZED DEPTH TO THE DISH'S FLAVOR PROFILE. LOOK FOR IT IN CHINESE MARKETS, AND IN A PINCH, SUBSTITUTE JAPANESE SAKE OR DRY SHERRY.

EQUIPMENT

YOU CAN MAKE DUMPLINGS WITHOUT A LOT OF SPECIAL EQUIPMENT, BUT THE KITCHEN ITEMS LISTED IN THIS SECTION COME IN QUITE HANDY TO FACILITATE THE PROCESS.

DEEP-FRY THERMOMETER

A DEEP-FRY THERMOMETER (ALSO CALLED A CANDY THERMOMETER) IS ESSENTIAL FOR DEEP-FRYING DUMPLINGS. THE OIL NEEDS TO STAY AT A STEADY, CONSISTENT HEAT THROUGHOUT THE PROCESS, AND A THERMOMETER ALLOWS YOU TO MONITOR THE HEAT AND ADJUST AS NECESSARY. OTHER THERMOMETERS WON'T READ HIGH ENOUGH TEMPERATURES OR HAVE THE METAL CLIP NECESSARY TO SECURE THE THERMOMETER TO THE SIDE OF YOUR POT. WHEN USING, BE SURE THE TIP OF THE THERMOMETER IS NOT TOUCHING THE BOTTOM OF THE POT SO YOU GET AN ACCURATE READING OF THE OIL TEMPERATURE!

BENCH SCRAPER

THE WIDE BLADE OF A BENCH SCRAPER HELPS YOU MOVE BIG PIECES OF DOUGH FROM ONE PLACE TO ANOTHER, IS FINE ENOUGH TO SCRAPE UP EXCESS DOUGH AND FLOUR DURING CLEANUP, AND IS SHARP ENOUGH TO CUT DOUGH FOR PORTIONING (BUT NOT SO SHARP THAT IT IS DANGEROUS TO HANDLE).

DUMPLING ROLLING PIN/ WOODEN DOWEL

A STANDARD-SIZED ROLLING PIN WILL WORK TO ROLL OUT DUMPLING WRAPPERS, BUT IT CAN GET A BIT CUMBERSOME. A SMALLER ROLLING PIN MADE SPECIFICALLY FOR DUMPLING WRAPPERS — OR EVEN A SIMPLE SMALL WOODEN DOWEL — IS MORE NIMBLE AND ADDS MORE FINESSE TO YOUR WRAPPER ROLLING GAME. NOTE THAT A PASTA ROLLER IS A VALUABLE UPGRADE WHEN ROLLING WONTON WRAPPERS (P. 31).

FISH SPATULA

THIS SLOTTED SPATULA IS GREAT FOR HANDLING PAN-FRIED DUMPLINGS, PICKING UP THE DUMPLING ITSELF WHILE LEAVING ANY EXCESS OIL BEHIND.

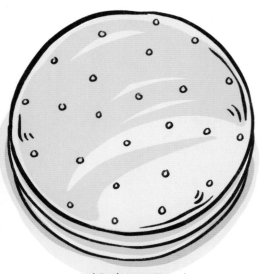

PARCHMENT PAPER

PARCHMENT PAPER IS AN INSTANT NONSTICK SURFACE FOR WRAPPER AND DUMPLING STAGING, AND IS PERFECT FOR KEEPING STEAMED BAO FROM STICKING TO THE STEAMER. THESE DAYS, PERFORATED PARCHMENT PAPER IS AVAILABLE FOR LINING STEAMERS SO THAT ALL THAT BEAUTIFUL STEAM CAN MAKE IT THROUGH TO COOK YOUR DUMPLINGS WITHOUT STICKING!

SHEET PAN

YOUR STANDARD BAKING SHEET IS GREAT TO HOLD WRAPPERS AND DUMPLINGS WHILE IN PRODUCTION MODE, IS EASY TO COVER WITH PLASTIC WRAP TO KEEP THEM FROM DRYING OUT DURING THE PROCESS, AND MAKES MOVING THEM ALL FROM ONE PLACE TO ANOTHER A CINCH.

STEAMERS

METAL STEAMERS CAN BE RIGGED TO SIT ABOVE BOILING WATER IN A POT OR WOK (THOUGH WE LIKE TO KEEP OUR WOKS WELL-SEASONED AND BOILING WATER CAN INTERFERE WITH THAT, SO WE STICK TO POTS!) AND SOMETIMES COME WITH BOTTOMS THAT CAN BE FILLED WITH WATER FOR STEAMING. BAMBOO STEAMERS CAN BE EASIER TO HANDLE AND IMPART A LOVELY AROMA TO THE AIR WHEN STEAMING DUMPLINGS. EITHER TYPE CAN BE STACKED AS HIGH AS IS SAFE, ALLOWING YOU TO COOK SEVERAL BATCHES OF DUMPLINGS AT ONCE, AND CAN DOUBLE AS SERVING VESSELS, MAKING THE TRANSFER FROM STOVE TO TABLE SEAMLESS.

SPIDER

A SPIDER IS LIKE A HAND-HELD COLANDER, MAKING IT EASY TO PLUCK DUMPLINGS FROM BOILING WATER OR HOT FRYER OIL.

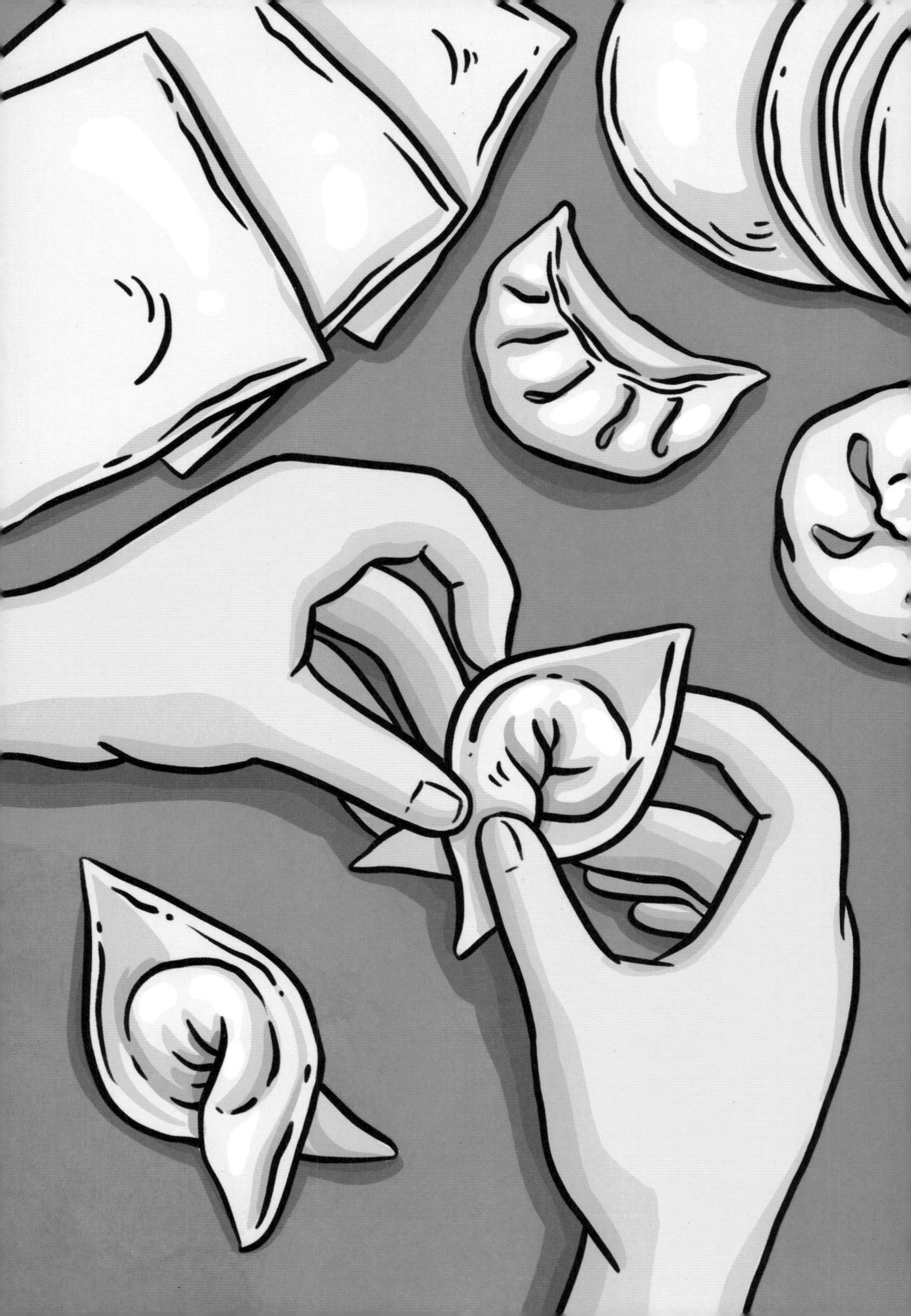

MAKING WRAPPERS & FOLDING DUMPLINGS

a word about
DUMPLING WRAPPERS

HOMEMADE DUMPLING WRAPPERS ARE TOTALLY WORTH THE EFFORT!

FOR SOMETHING WITH SUCH A DEEP, WHEATY AROMA AND SATISFYING, CHEWY TEXTURE,

THEY ARE INCREDIBLY SIMPLE TO MAKE — ESSENTIALLY, JUST MIX TOGETHER A BIT OF FLOUR AND WATER.

SPECIALIZED DUMPLING FLOUR ISN'T NECESSARY FOR OUR SAVORY DUMPLING AND WONTON WRAPPERS —

THE PROTEIN CONTENT OF ALL-PURPOSE FLOUR BUILDS A STURDY GLUTEN NETWORK FOR STRONG, CHEWY WRAPPERS.

VETERAN DUMPLING MAKERS HAVE PLENTIFUL OPINIONS ON WATER TEMPERATURE FOR MAKING WRAPPERS:

BOILING WATER CAUSES THE STARCH IN THE DOUGH TO GELATE,

MAKING THE DOUGH SOFTER, SIMPLER TO WORK WITH, AND EASY TO ROLL THINLY (GOOD FOR FRIED AND STEAMED DUMPLINGS),

WHILE COOL WATER WILL RESULT IN STRONGER WRAPPERS (GOOD FOR BOILED DUMPLINGS).

FOR SIMPLICITY'S SAKE, WE LAND SOMEWHERE IN BETWEEN, POURING BOILING WATER INTO A MEASURING CUP CONTAINING THE RECIPE'S SALT,

WHICH COOLS THE WATER A BIT AND DISSOLVES THE SALT ALONG THE WAY.

DON'T SKIP THE DOUGH'S 30-MINUTE REST—

AND DON'T OVERHANDLE OR PLAY AROUND WITH IT TOO MUCH WHILE ROLLING IT OUT!

THE REST AND GENTLE TREATMENT LETS THE NOW-DEVELOPED GLUTEN IN THE DOUGH RELAX, MAKING IT EASIER TO ROLL OUT NICE AND THIN.

USE A PASTA ROLLER TO ROLL THE DOUGH OUT INTO ONE BIG SHEET

TO BE CUT INTO SQUARES FOR WONTON WRAPPERS.

FOR ROUND DUMPLING WRAPPERS, WE FIND THE MINIMALIST APPROACH OF CUTTING AND ROLLING EACH WRAPPER INDIVIDUALLY IS ACTUALLY EASIER,

LESS CUMBERSOME,

AND YIELDS BETTER RESULTS.

BUT AS ALWAYS, DO WHAT FEELS RIGHT FOR YOU!

DUMPLING WRAPPERS

MAKES ABOUT 48 WRAPPERS

INGREDIENTS:

600 GRAMS (ABOUT 4 CUPS) ALL-PURPOSE FLOUR, PLUS MORE FOR DUSTING

2 TEASPOONS SALT

BOILING WATER

PLACE FLOUR IN A LARGE BOWL

AND POUR THE SALT INTO A GLASS MEASURING CUP OF AT LEAST 2-CUP CAPACITY.

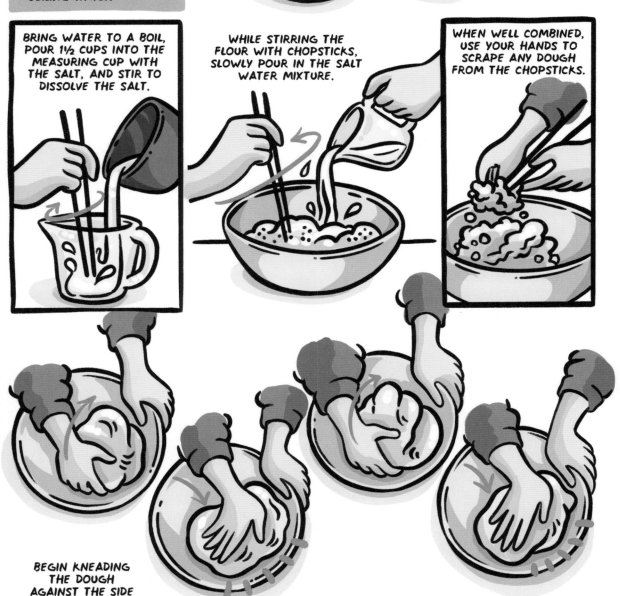

BRING WATER TO A BOIL, POUR 1½ CUPS INTO THE MEASURING CUP WITH THE SALT, AND STIR TO DISSOLVE THE SALT.

WHILE STIRRING THE FLOUR WITH CHOPSTICKS, SLOWLY POUR IN THE SALT WATER MIXTURE.

WHEN WELL COMBINED, USE YOUR HANDS TO SCRAPE ANY DOUGH FROM THE CHOPSTICKS.

BEGIN KNEADING THE DOUGH AGAINST THE SIDE OF THE BOWL.

WHEN THE DOUGH IS IN ONE COHESIVE PIECE, AND ALL THE CRUMBS AND FLOUR HAVE BEEN INCORPORATED,

CONTINUE KNEADING UNTIL THE DOUGH IS SMOOTH, 2 TO 3 MINUTES.

WRAP TIGHTLY IN
PLASTIC WRAP

AND LET REST FOR
30 MINUTES AT ROOM
TEMPERATURE,

OR REFRIGERATE FOR UP
TO 1 DAY, LETTING THE
DOUGH SIT AT ROOM
TEMPERATURE FOR 30
MINUTES BEFORE USING.

WHEN YOU ARE
READY TO ROLL
YOUR WRAPPERS,
CUT THE DOUGH
BALL IN QUARTERS.

KEEP THREE QUARTERS
COVERED AND ROLL ONE
QUARTER INTO A LOG
ABOUT 1 FOOT LONG.

CUT THE DOUGH INTO
TWELVE EQUAL PIECES.

WE LIKE TO
CUT THE LOG
IN HALF,

THEN CUT EACH
HALF IN HALF
AGAIN TO GET
FOUR EQUAL PIECES.

FROM THERE IT'S
EASIER TO CUT EACH
LENGTH INTO THREE
EQUAL PIECES

FOR A TOTAL OF
TWELVE EVENLY SIZED
PIECES OF DOUGH.

STAND EACH
DOUGH PIECE ON
ITS CUT SIDE,

GIVE IT A LITTLE
PINCH TO SHAPE IT
INTO A DISC,

AND FLATTEN IT AS
MUCH AS POSSIBLE
WITH THE HEEL OF
YOUR HAND.

USING A SMALL WOODEN DOWEL (SEE EQUIPMENT, P. 20) OR A ROLLING PIN,

ROLL EACH PIECE OF DOUGH INTO A ROUND ABOUT 3½ INCHES IN DIAMETER AND ABOUT ⅛ INCH THICK,

ROTATING THE DOUGH AFTER EACH ROLL AND DUSTING LIGHTLY WITH FLOUR AS NEEDED TO PREVENT STICKING.

DON'T STRESS TOO MUCH ABOUT MAKING THEM PERFECT CIRCLES!

RATHER THAN FREEZING THE DOUGH BALLS OR WRAPPERS, THESE WRAPPERS ARE BEST FILLED AND SHAPED BEFORE FREEZING!

LIGHTLY DUST THE WRAPPERS WITH FLOUR AND SHINGLE ON A LIGHTLY FLOURED SHEET PAN

AND KEEP THEM COVERED WITH PLASTIC WRAP WHEN NOT IN USE (WRAPPERS CAN BE REFRIGERATED UP TO 4 HOURS).

WHEN READY TO USE, PROCEED TO FILL, WRAP, AND COOK AS DIRECTED LATER IN THIS CHAPTER AND UNDER COOKING DUMPLINGS (P. 47).

a word about
WONTON WRAPPERS

WONTON WRAPPERS ARE THINNER THAN DUMPLING WRAPPERS AND VERY PASTA-LIKE, USUALLY INCLUDING AN EGG,

THE FAT OF WHICH NOT ONLY BOOSTS RICHNESS,

BUT SLIGHTLY INHIBITS GLUTEN DEVELOPMENT AND MAKES THE DOUGH EASIER TO ROLL OUT.

ROLL THESE WRAPPERS THIN ENOUGH TO SEE THE OUTLINE OF YOUR FINGERS THROUGH WHEN HOLDING THE DOUGH.

WE HIGHLY RECOMMEND USING A PASTA MACHINE.

WONTON WRAPPERS

INGREDIENTS:

300 GRAMS (ABOUT 2 CUPS) ALL-PURPOSE FLOUR, PLUS MORE FOR DUSTING

1 TEASPOON SALT

1 LARGE EGG

½ CUP WATER, AT ROOM TEMPERATURE

PLACE THE FLOUR AND SALT IN A MEDIUM BOWL AND STIR TO COMBINE.

FORM A WELL IN THE MIDDLE OF THE FLOUR AND ADD THE EGG AND WATER.

STIR WITH CHOPSTICKS

AND WHEN COMBINED, USE YOUR HANDS TO SCRAPE EXCESS DOUGH FROM THE CHOPSTICKS,

AND BEGIN KNEADING THE DOUGH AGAINST THE SIDE OF THE BOWL.

WHEN THE DOUGH IS ONE COHESIVE PIECE, AND ALL CRUMBS AND FLOUR HAVE BEEN INCORPORATED,

CONTINUE KNEADING UNTIL THE DOUGH IS SMOOTH, 2 TO 3 MINUTES.

WRAP TIGHTLY IN PLASTIC WRAP AND LET REST FOR 30 MINUTES AT ROOM TEMPERATURE,

OR REFRIGERATE FOR UP TO 1 DAY, LETTING THE DOUGH SIT AT ROOM TEMPERATURE FOR 30 MINUTES BEFORE USING.

WHEN YOU ARE READY TO ROLL YOUR WRAPPERS, SET UP A PASTA MACHINE AND MAKE SURE IT IS ON THE THICKEST SETTING.

CUT THE DOUGH BALL IN HALF AND KEEP THE OTHER HALF COVERED.

YOU CAN ALSO USE A ROLLING PIN,

JUST BE AWARE THAT IT WILL TAKE A LOT OF PATIENCE AND STRENGTH

FLATTEN THE UNCOVERED HALF AS MUCH AS POSSIBLE WITH YOUR HAND.

DUSTING LIGHTLY WITH FLOUR AS NEEDED,

TO ROLL THE DOUGH TO BE AS THIN AS REQUIRED,

SO BE SURE TO LET THE DOUGH REST NOW AND THEN TO RELAX THE GLUTEN AND MAKE IT EASIER TO ROLL.

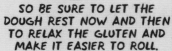

CRANK THE DOUGH THROUGH THE PASTA MACHINE.

BUMP THE MACHINE'S THICKNESS DOWN A NOTCH, AND ROLL THE DOUGH THROUGH AGAIN.

REPEAT THIS PROCESS UNTIL YOU ARE ONE OR TWO NOTCHES AWAY FROM THE THINNEST SETTING,

AND YOU CAN EASILY SEE THE OUTLINE OF YOUR FINGERS THROUGH THE SHEET OF DOUGH.

SET ASIDE, COVER WITH PLASTIC, AND REPEAT WITH THE REMAINING DOUGH HALF.

CUT THE DOUGH INTO APPROXIMATELY 3 BY 3-INCH SQUARES.

DUST THE CUT WRAPPERS WITH FLOUR AND SHINGLE ON A LIGHTLY FLOURED SHEET PAN

AND KEEP THEM COVERED WITH PLASTIC WRAP WHEN NOT IN USE (WRAPPERS CAN BE REFRIGERATED UP TO 4 HOURS).

REPEAT THE PROCESS WITH THE REMAINING DOUGH.

RATHER THAN FREEZING THE DOUGH BALLS OR WRAPPERS, THESE WRAPPERS ARE BEST FILLED AND SHAPED BEFORE FREEZING!

WHEN READY TO USE, PROCEED TO FILL, FOLD, AND COOK AS DIRECTED FOR WONTONS (P. 40) AND UNDER COOKING DUMPLINGS (P. 47).

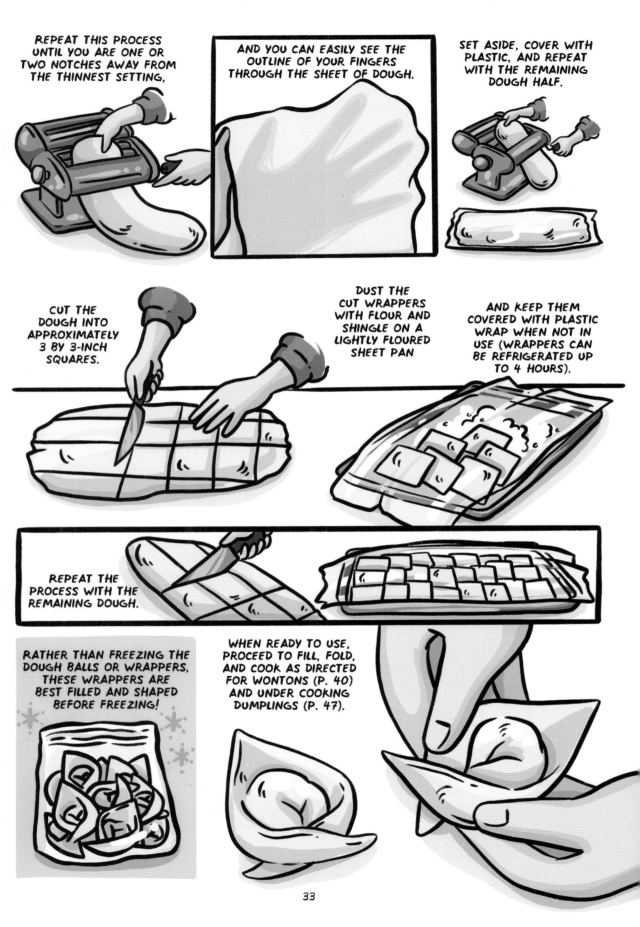

HALF-MOON

LIGHTLY WET THE ENTIRE RIM OF A DUMPLING WRAPPER WITH WATER USING YOUR PINKY, KEEPING YOUR OTHER FINGERS DRY.

FOLD IN HALF LIKE A TACO

AND PINCH THE ENDS TOGETHER.

WORK FROM THE MIDDLE TO SEAL HALF OF THE DUMPLING

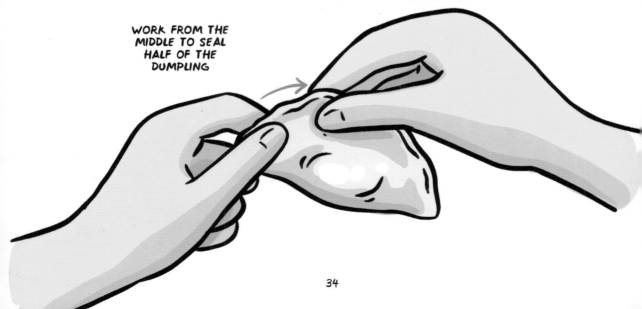

THEN SEAL THE OTHER HALF, MAKING SURE TO REMOVE AS MUCH AIR AS POSSIBLE BEFORE YOU FINISH SEALING,

AND FLATTEN A BIT ON THE BOTTOM.

PLEATED CRESCENT

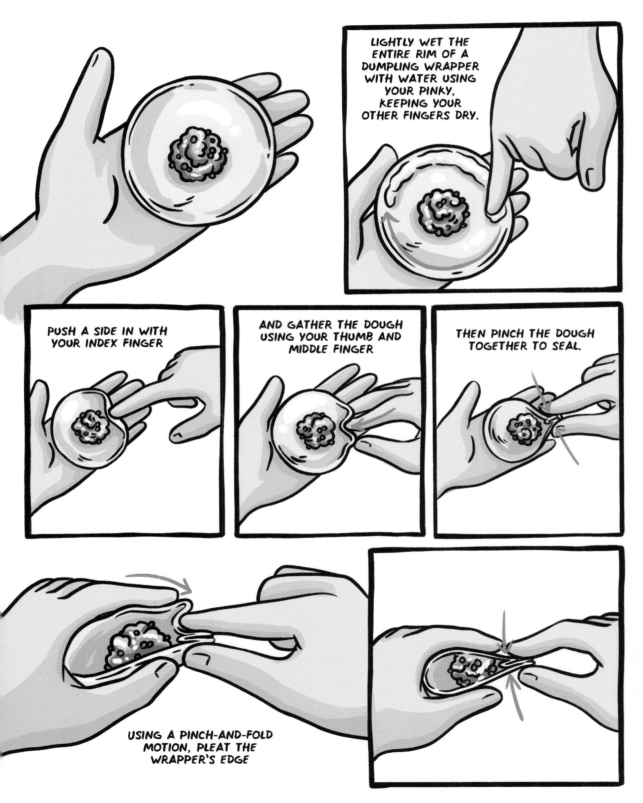

LIGHTLY WET THE ENTIRE RIM OF A DUMPLING WRAPPER WITH WATER USING YOUR PINKY, KEEPING YOUR OTHER FINGERS DRY.

PUSH A SIDE IN WITH YOUR INDEX FINGER

AND GATHER THE DOUGH USING YOUR THUMB AND MIDDLE FINGER

THEN PINCH THE DOUGH TOGETHER TO SEAL.

USING A PINCH-AND-FOLD MOTION, PLEAT THE WRAPPER'S EDGE

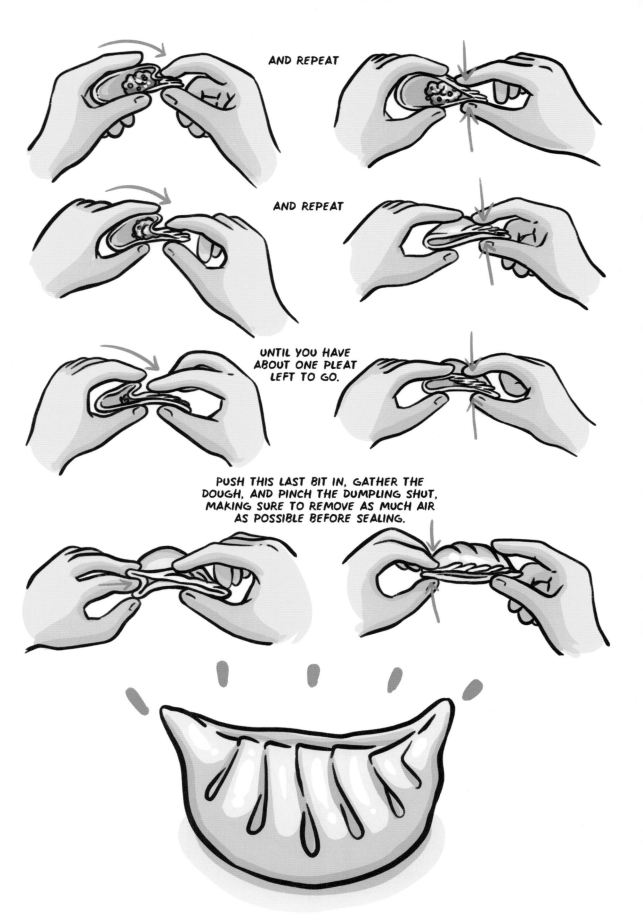

AND REPEAT

AND REPEAT

UNTIL YOU HAVE
ABOUT ONE PLEAT
LEFT TO GO.

PUSH THIS LAST BIT IN, GATHER THE
DOUGH, AND PINCH THE DUMPLING SHUT,
MAKING SURE TO REMOVE AS MUCH AIR
AS POSSIBLE BEFORE SEALING.

TRIANGLE

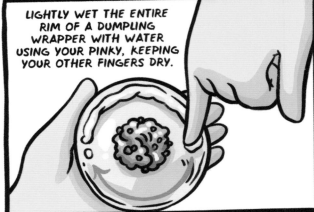

LIGHTLY WET THE ENTIRE RIM OF A DUMPLING WRAPPER WITH WATER USING YOUR PINKY, KEEPING YOUR OTHER FINGERS DRY.

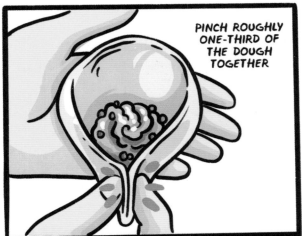

PINCH ROUGHLY ONE-THIRD OF THE DOUGH TOGETHER

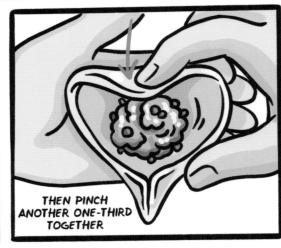

THEN PINCH ANOTHER ONE-THIRD TOGETHER

THEN PINCH THE OTHER ONE-THIRD IN, MAKING SURE TO REMOVE AS MUCH AIR AS POSSIBLE, AND PRESS ALL EDGES TOGETHER TO SECURE THE SEAL.

4-POINTED STAR

LIGHTLY WET THE ENTIRE RIM OF A WONTON WRAPPER WITH WATER USING YOUR PINKY, KEEPING YOUR OTHER FINGERS DRY.

PINCH 2 OPPOSITE CORNERS, SEALING THE FLAT PART OF THE WRAPPER BUT LEAVING A BIT UNSEALED OUT TOWARD THE CORNER.

PRESS THE WRAPPER IN TO MEET IN THE CENTER OF THE DUMPLING

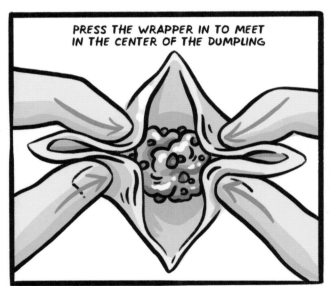

MAKING SURE THE FILLING IS SEALED IN COMPLETELY

BUT THE CORNERS ARE LEFT OPEN FOR MORE CRISPY SURFACE AREA WHEN FRYING.

WONTON

LIGHTLY WET THE ENTIRE RIM OF A WONTON WRAPPER WITH WATER USING YOUR PINKY, KEEPING YOUR OTHER FINGERS DRY.

FOLD WRAPPER UP TO MAKE A TRIANGLE.

SEAL, MAKING SURE TO REMOVE AS MUCH AIR AS POSSIBLE.

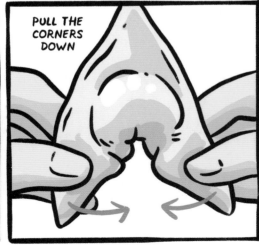

PULL THE CORNERS DOWN

AND WET THE TOP OF ONE CORNER.

PRESS THE OPPOSITE CORNER ONTO THE WET CORNER TO ADHERE.

MOMO

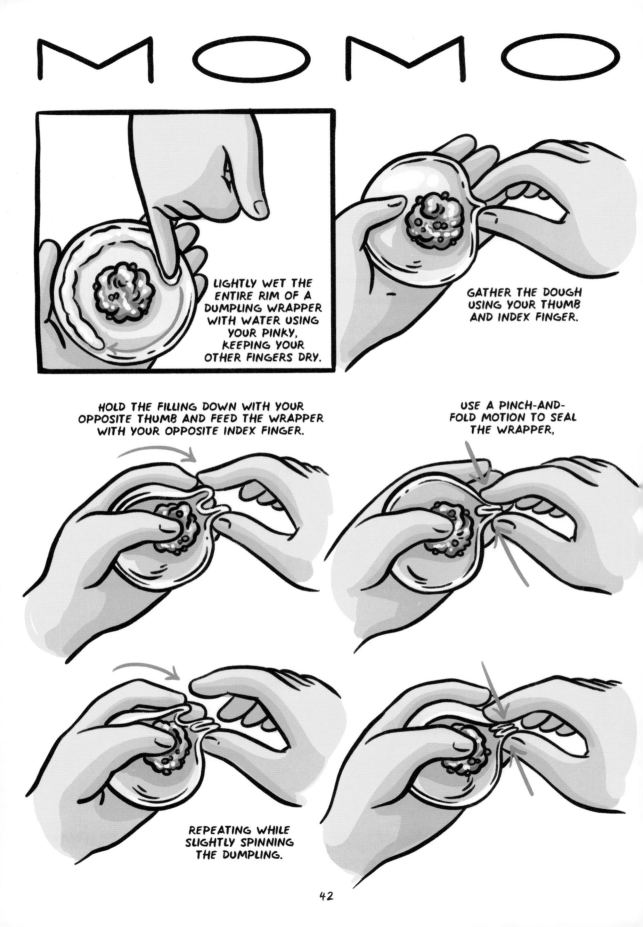

LIGHTLY WET THE ENTIRE RIM OF A DUMPLING WRAPPER WITH WATER USING YOUR PINKY, KEEPING YOUR OTHER FINGERS DRY.

GATHER THE DOUGH USING YOUR THUMB AND INDEX FINGER.

HOLD THE FILLING DOWN WITH YOUR OPPOSITE THUMB AND FEED THE WRAPPER WITH YOUR OPPOSITE INDEX FINGER.

USE A PINCH-AND-FOLD MOTION TO SEAL THE WRAPPER,

REPEATING WHILE SLIGHTLY SPINNING THE DUMPLING.

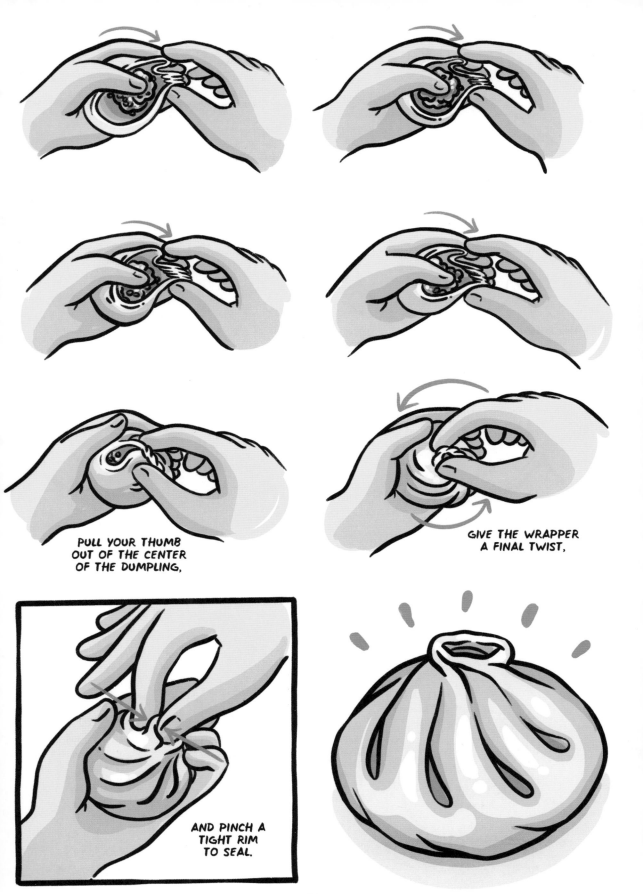

PULL YOUR THUMB
OUT OF THE CENTER
OF THE DUMPLING,

GIVE THE WRAPPER
A FINAL TWIST,

AND PINCH A
TIGHT RIM
TO SEAL.

SHUMAI

LIGHTLY WET THE ENTIRE RIM OF A DUMPLING WRAPPER WITH WATER USING YOUR PINKY, KEEPING YOUR OTHER FINGERS DRY.

CUP THE DUMPLING BETWEEN YOUR INDEX FINGER AND THUMB TO FORM AN "O"

AND PUSH THE FILLING DOWN INTO THE WRAPPER.

PRESS THE WRAPPER AROUND THE FILLING TO MAKE A BASKET.

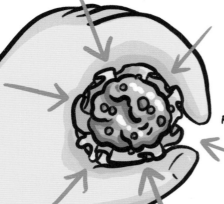

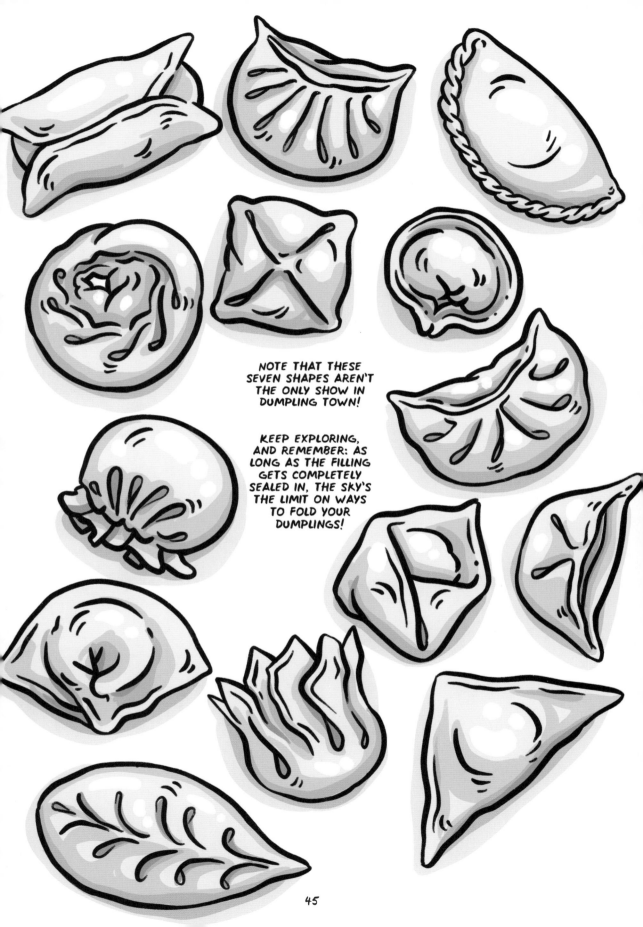

NOTE THAT THESE SEVEN SHAPES AREN'T THE ONLY SHOW IN DUMPLING TOWN!

KEEP EXPLORING, AND REMEMBER: AS LONG AS THE FILLING GETS COMPLETELY SEALED IN, THE SKY'S THE LIMIT ON WAYS TO FOLD YOUR DUMPLINGS!

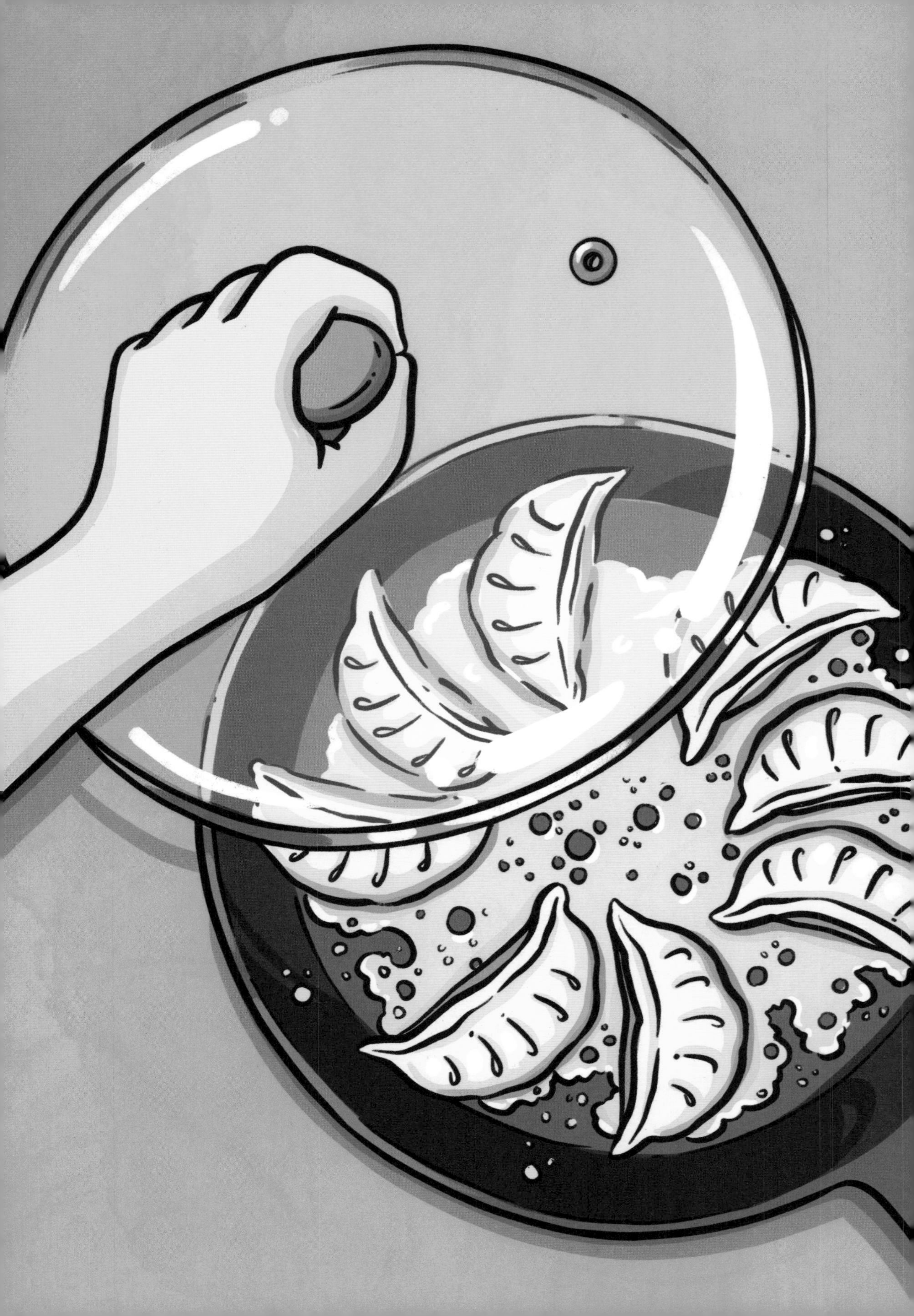

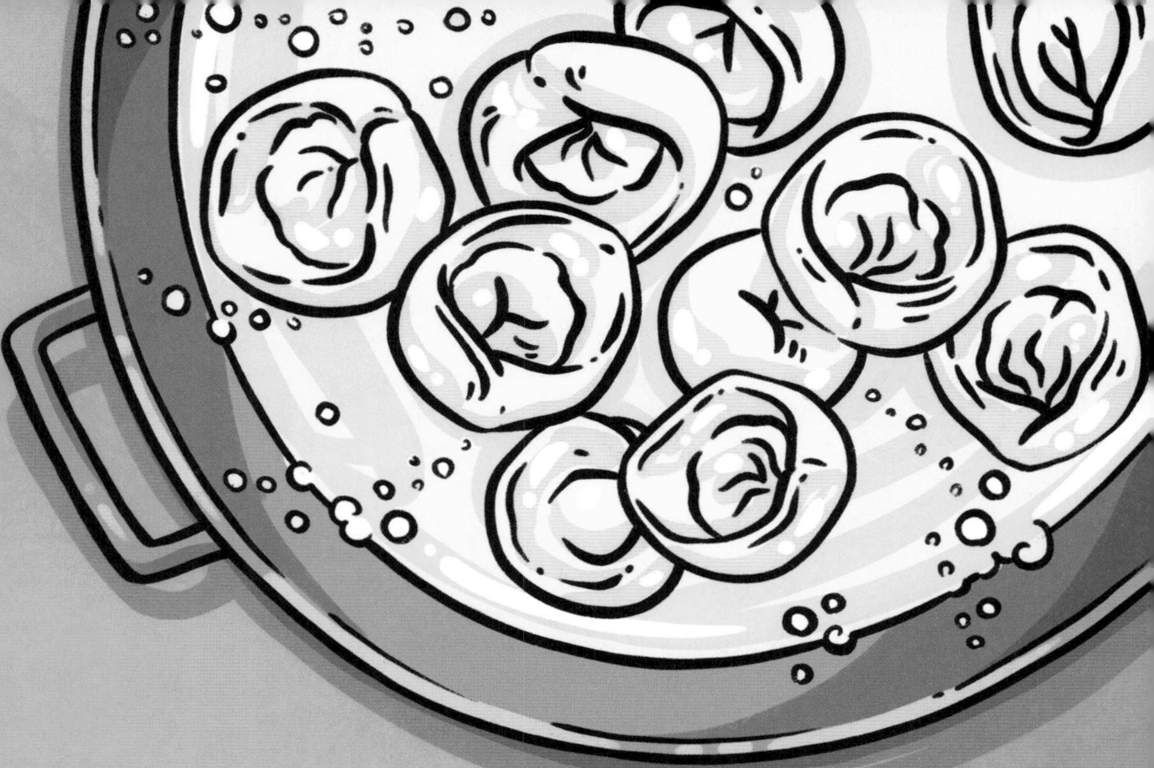

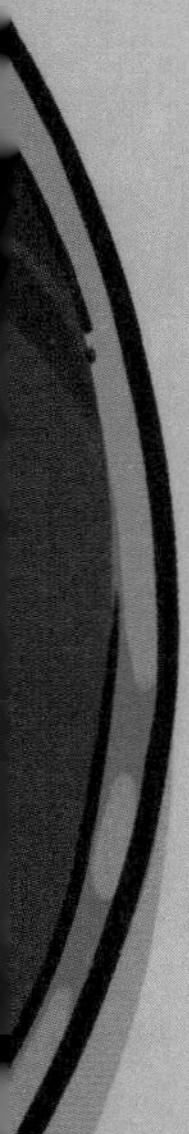

COOKING DUMPLINGS

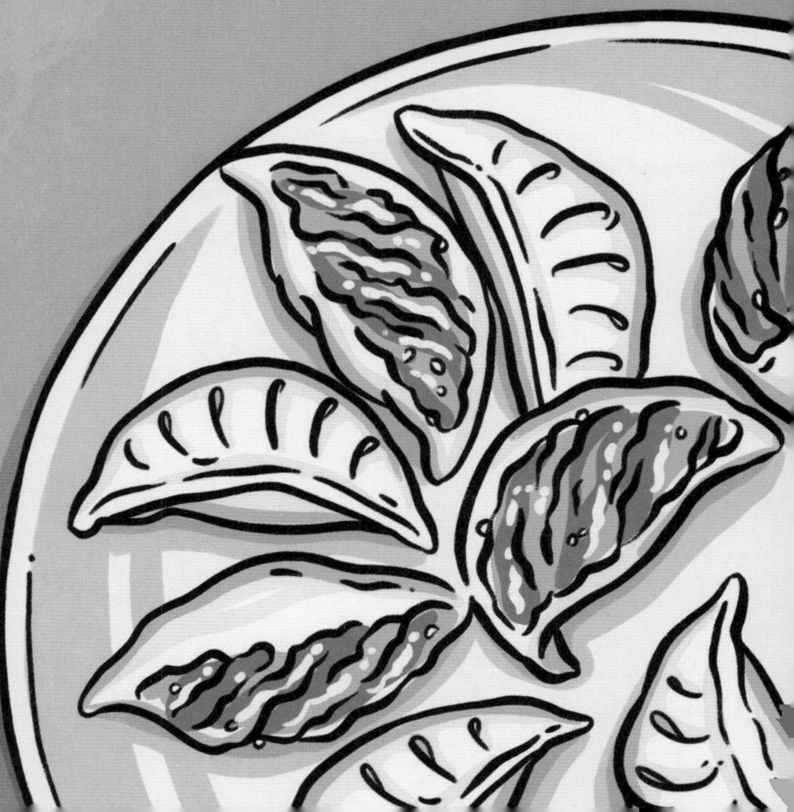

a word about COOKING DUMPLINGS

VARIETY IN THE WORLD OF DUMPLINGS DOESN'T STOP AT FILLINGS, SHAPES, AND SIZES —

SEVERAL COOKING TECHNIQUES CAN BE APPLIED WITH GREAT SUCCESS, EACH BRINGING THEIR OWN SPECIAL ATTRIBUTES TO THE TABLE.

ONE OF THE BEAUTIFUL THINGS ABOUT DUMPLINGS IS THAT THEY CAN BE COMPLETELY PREPPED IN ADVANCE OF MEALTIME (AND SOMETIMES EVEN FROZEN) AND COOKED TO ORDER,

MOVING FROM STOVE TO TABLE TO MOUTH IN A MATTER OF MINUTES, MAKING FOR AN ENTERTAINING AND INTERACTIVE DINNER PARTY OR A QUICK WEEKNIGHT MEAL!

IN THIS BOOK, WE SUGGEST COOKING TECHNIQUES, BUT REMEMBER: IN MOST CASES, IT'S UP TO YOU!

IF YOU FAVOR ONE OF THESE TECHNIQUES OVER ANOTHER, BY ALL MEANS GIVE IT A GO

AS LONG AS YOU PAY HEED TO ANY LIMITATIONS —

YOU WOULDN'T WANT TO DEEP FRY AN OPEN-TOPPED SHUMAI!

JUST BE SURE TO HAVE YOUR EQUIPMENT, SAUCES, AND TABLE READY TO GO —

A HOT DUMPLING WAITS FOR NO ONE!

BOILING DUMPLINGS

PROBABLY THE EASIEST, LOWEST MAINTENANCE DUMPLING-COOKING TECHNIQUE,

BOILING JUST REQUIRES A BIG POT AND A SPIDER OR COLANDER.

BOILING WORKS BEST WITH THICKER-SKINNED DUMPLINGS THAT CAN WITHSTAND BEING TOSSED AROUND IN HOT WATER FOR A FEW MINUTES,

AND THOUGH YOU WON'T GET THE CRISPY WRAPPER THAT COMES WITH FRIED DUMPLINGS, BOILING GIVES YOU A GREAT STEAMED-WHEAT AROMA,

AND ONCE THAT EXCESS MOISTURE STEAMS AWAY, A TEXTURE PERFECT FOR SAUCE TO ADHERE TO WHEN DIPPING.

USE A BIG POT WITH PLENTY OF WATER, AND DON'T OVERFILL IT WITH DUMPLINGS LEST YOU COOL THE WATER DOWN, MAKING IT HARD TO RECOVER THE BOIL.

WORK IN BATCHES IF NECESSARY TO KEEP THE WATER HOT AND BOILING, AND BE SURE TO ADJUST THE HEAT TO MAINTAIN A GENTLE BOIL WITHOUT A STARCHY BOILOVER!

THERE'S NO NEED TO SALT THE WATER SINCE THE DUMPLINGS (AND THE SAUCES THEY ARE GOING TO BE DIPPED IN) ARE ALREADY HIGHLY SEASONED!

TO BOIL DUMPLINGS:

BRING A LARGE POT WITH AT LEAST 4 QUARTS OF WATER TO A BOIL OVER HIGH HEAT.

GENTLY SWIRL THE WATER WITH A SPIDER TO KEEP IT MOVING

SOME RECIPES WILL TELL YOU THAT WHEN THE DUMPLINGS FLOAT, THEY ARE DONE.

AS YOU CAREFULLY DROP THE DUMPLINGS IN ONE AT A TIME.

COOK FOR 5 TO 8 MINUTES (8 TO 10 MINUTES IF FROZEN), STIRRING OCCASIONALLY TO PREVENT STICKING,

THIS CAN BE MISLEADING IF ALL OF THE AIR WASN'T REMOVED FROM YOUR DUMPLINGS BEFORE THEY WERE SEALED, SO BE SURE THEY ARE COOKED THROUGH BEFORE FISHING THEM OUT OF THE BOILING WATER!

UNTIL THE FILLING IS COOKED THROUGH AND THE DOUGH IS EVER SO SLIGHTLY TRANSLUCENT.

REMOVE FROM THE POT USING A SPIDER, SHAKING EXCESS WATER FROM THE DUMPLINGS,

AND PLACE THEM IN A SERVING DISH. SERVE IMMEDIATELY WITH A SAUCE AS SUGGESTED IN YOUR RECIPE.

STEAMING DUMPLINGS

STEAMING IS ANOTHER QUICK AND EASY METHOD FOR COOKING DUMPLINGS,

GREAT FOR YEAST-RISEN BAO, OPEN-TOPPED SHUMAI,

AND ANY OTHER DUMPLINGS WITH FEATURES THAT REQUIRE GENTLE HANDLING.

PLUS, IF YOU USE MULTI-TIERED STEAMER BASKETS, YOU CAN COOK A TON OF DUMPLINGS AT ONCE —

JUST BE SURE TO GIVE THEM SPACE IN EACH BASKET TO KEEP THEM FROM STICKING TO EACH OTHER!

STEAMING EQUIPMENT MAY LOOK COMPLICATED, BUT IT IS QUITE SIMPLE TO ACQUIRE AND USE (SEE EQUIPMENT, P. 21)

AND CAN BE PUT TO USE BEYOND DUMPLINGS (STEAMING FISH, POULTRY, AND VEGETABLES ARE ALL GREAT APPLICATIONS).

ALWAYS EXERCISE CAUTION WHEN WORKING WITH A STEAMER — STEAM BURNS ARE VICIOUS!

OPEN THE STEAMER BASKET AWAY FROM YOURSELF AND OTHERS AND BE AWARE OF WHERE THE STEAM IS SHOOTING.

AND DON'T SKIP THE PARCHMENT PAPER OR CABBAGE LINERS — ESSENTIAL FOR MAKING SURE NOTHING STICKS TO THE STEAMER BASKETS!

TO STEAM DUMPLINGS:

FILL YOUR STEAMER OR HEAVY POT WITH A COUPLE OF INCHES OF WATER — IF USING A WOK, FILL WITH ENOUGH WATER TO SUBMERGE THE BOTTOM RIM OF YOUR STEAMER BASKETS WITHOUT TOUCHING THE BED ON WHICH THE FOOD IS COOKING —

AND BRING TO A BOIL OVER HIGH HEAT.

MEANWHILE, LINE YOUR STEAMER BASKETS WITH PERFORATED PARCHMENT PAPER OR NAPA CABBAGE LEAVES

BEFORE PLACING THE DUMPLINGS ON TOP, LEAVING ABOUT ½ INCH OF SPACE AROUND EACH DUMPLING TO ALLOW FOR STEAM FLOW.

(NOTE: BAOZI MUST BE ALLOWED TO RISE AT THIS POINT — SEE BAOZI, P. 121)

WHEN THE WATER IN THE STEAMER IS BOILING, CAREFULLY PLACE THE STEAMER BASKETS IN THE STEAMER,

STACKING AS MANY TIERS AS YOU HAVE FILLED, AND COVER WITH THE LID.

STEAM UNTIL THE DUMPLINGS ARE COOKED THROUGH AND THE DOUGH IS SLIGHTLY TRANSLUCENT, 8 TO 10 MINUTES (10 TO 12 MINUTES IF FROZEN),

MAKING SURE THE WATER BOILS CONTINUOUSLY IN A CONTROLLED FASHION.

WHEN THE DUMPLINGS ARE COOKED, CAREFULLY REMOVE THE LID OF THE STEAMER

AND SERVE IMMEDIATELY IN THE STEAMER BASKET WITH A SAUCE AS SUGGESTED IN YOUR RECIPE.

PAN-FRYING DUMPLINGS

PAN-FRYING DUMPLINGS (ALSO KNOWN AS THE POTSTICKER TECHNIQUE) YIELDS THE BEST OF BOTH TEXTURE WORLDS:

CRISPY AND GOLDEN BROWN, SOFT AND CHEWY ALL IN ONE DUMPLING!

SURE, IT CAN GET A BIT MESSY AND DANGEROUS WHAT WITH WATER BEING POURED INTO A PAN OF HOT OIL, BUT THE FLAVOR PAYOFF IS WELL WORTH IT.

STAY FOCUSED AS YOU POUR THE WATER INTO THE PAN, USING THE LID AS A SHIELD AND MAKING SURE THE HOT OIL AND STEAM STAY DIRECTED AWAY FROM YOU AND OTHERS.

IF YOUR PAN DOESN'T HAVE A LID, SIMPLY USE A BAKING SHEET OR LARGE PIECE OF ALUMINUM FOIL TO COVER YOUR PAN!

WE RECOMMEND NONSTICK PANS FOR EASIEST RESULTS, BUT WELL-SEASONED CAST IRON WORKS GREAT, TOO.

TO PAN-FRY DUMPLINGS:

HEAT A 10-INCH OR LARGER NONSTICK OR CAST-IRON PAN OVER MEDIUM-HIGH HEAT

ADD A COUPLE OF TABLESPOONS OF A NEUTRAL OIL, AND SWIRL IT AROUND THE PAN.

LAY YOUR DUMPLINGS IN THE PAN ON THEIR FLATTEST SIDE, LEAVING ABOUT ½ INCH OF SPACE AROUND EACH DUMPLING TO ALLOW FOR STEAM FLOW.

FRY UNTIL THE BOTTOMS OF THE DUMPLINGS ARE LIGHTLY GOLDEN BROWN (USE A FISH SPATULA OR FORK TO LIFT A DUMPLING UP FOR A PEEK), ABOUT 2 MINUTES.

HOLDING THE PAN'S LID (OR A BAKING SHEET) NEAR THE PAN TO SERVE AS A SHIELD, POUR ½ CUP OF WATER INTO THE PAN

AND COVER IMMEDIATELY (THE WATER WILL SPUTTER AND SPIT FURIOUSLY!).

LOWER THE HEAT TO MEDIUM AND LET COOK, TIGHTLY COVERED, FOR 5 MINUTES MORE.

LOOSEN THE LID SO IT IS SLIGHTLY AJAR TO LET THE STEAM ESCAPE. COOK FOR ANOTHER 2 TO 3 MINUTES, UNTIL MOST OF THE WATER IS GONE,

THEN REMOVE THE LID COMPLETELY AND LET THE DUMPLINGS FINISH FRYING FOR ANOTHER MINUTE OR SO,

UNTIL GOLDEN BROWN ON THE BOTTOM AND THE FILLING IS COOKED THROUGH.

USING YOUR FISH SPATULA TO LEAVE AS MUCH OIL BEHIND AS POSSIBLE, TRANSFER THE DUMPLINGS TO A SERVING PLATE

AND SERVE IMMEDIATELY WITH A SAUCE AS SUGGESTED IN YOUR RECIPE.

DEEP-FRYING DUMPLINGS

DEEP-FRYING DUMPLINGS IS SIMPLY INDULGENT.

THE CRISPY WRAPPER JUXTAPOSED AGAINST THE SOFT, STEAMY FILLING IS ONE OF THE GREAT TEXTURAL PLEASURES OF THE CULINARY WORLD!

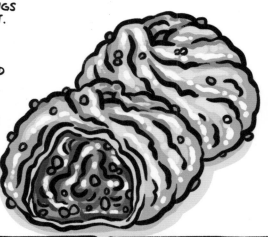

WE LIKE USING INEXPENSIVE CANOLA OIL FOR ITS HIGH SMOKE POINT AND NEUTRAL FLAVOR — PEANUT OIL IS GREAT AS WELL THOUGH MORE EXPENSIVE.

AS ALWAYS, WHEN WORKING WITH HOT OIL, EXERCISE GREAT CAUTION.

DON'T OVERFILL THE POT WITH OIL (KEEPING IT A THIRD FULL OR LESS IS IDEAL),

BE AWARE OF THE POT AND ITS POSITION ON THE STOVE WHEN COMPLETING OTHER TASKS,

AND HAVE COOLING RACKS AND SERVING PLATTERS READY TO GO.

ALSO, A GOOD DEEP-FRY THERMOMETER IS ESSENTIAL TO KEEP THE OIL AT THE PROPER TEMPERATURE.

OIL THAT IS TOO COOL WILL PRODUCE SOGGY, OILY DUMPLINGS, AND OIL THAT IS TOO HOT WILL BURN THE DUMPLING WRAPPERS BEFORE THE FILLING HAS A CHANCE TO COOK THROUGH!

BE SURE TO WORK IN APPROPRIATELY SIZED BATCHES (AT LEAST HALF OF THE AREA OF THE BOTTOM OF THE PAN SHOULD REMAIN VISIBLE AT ALL TIMES) SO THE OIL MAINTAINS ITS PROPER TEMPERATURE.

TO DEEP-FRY DUMPLINGS:

SET A COOLING RACK ON A SHEET PAN AND SET NEXT TO YOUR FRYING SETUP WITH A SPIDER AT THE READY.

HEAT ABOUT 2 INCHES OF NEUTRAL OIL IN A HEAVY POT OF ABOUT 5-QUART CAPACITY OVER HIGH HEAT

(THIS SIZE CAN VARY, JUST ADJUST THE AMOUNT OF OIL AND BATCH SIZE ACCORDINGLY).

USING A DEEP-FRY THERMOMETER

(BE SURE THE THERMOMETER ISN'T TOUCHING THE BOTTOM OF THE PAN AND MEASURING THE TEMPERATURE OF THE METAL!),

HEAT THE OIL TO 375°F

(YOU ULTIMATELY WANT TO MAINTAIN A HEAT OF 350°F, BUT START WITH A HIGHER TEMPERATURE SINCE THE OIL'S TEMPERATURE WILL DROP WHEN DUMPLINGS ARE ADDED).

CAREFULLY DROP ABOUT SIX DUMPLINGS INTO THE OIL (OR AS MANY AS YOUR POT CAN ACCOMMODATE WHILE MAINTAINING PROPER TEMPERATURE)

AND WATCH THE OIL'S TEMPERATURE, ADJUSTING THE HEAT AS NECESSARY TO MAINTAIN 350°F.

FRY, STIRRING OCCASIONALLY, UNTIL WRAPPERS ARE GOLDEN BROWN AND FILLING IS COOKED THROUGH, ABOUT 2 MINUTES.

IF THE WRAPPERS LOOK LIKE THEY COULD BURN BEFORE THE FILLING IS COOKED THROUGH, PLACE THE DUMPLINGS ON A BAKING SHEET AND FINISH COOKING IN A 350°F OVEN FOR ABOUT 5 MINUTES.

USE A SPIDER TO TRANSFER THE COOKED DUMPLINGS TO THE COOLING RACK AS YOU FRY SUBSEQUENT BATCHES.

THEN, JUST BEFORE SERVING, FLASH FRY THE DUMPLINGS FOR A FEW SECONDS TO RE-CRISP THE WRAPPERS.

WHEN YOU ARE READY TO SERVE, TRANSFER THE DUMPLINGS TO A SERVING PLATE AND SERVE IMMEDIATELY WITH A SAUCE AS SUGGESTED IN YOUR RECIPE.

FREEZING DUMPLINGS

PREPPING A TON OF DUMPLINGS AND THEN FREEZING THEM IS A GREAT WAY TO HAVE QUICK DINNERS (OR A PARTY!) IN YOUR FREEZER, READY TO GO AT ANY TIME.

AFTER ALL, IF YOU ARE GOING TO BE MAKING DUMPLINGS, YOU MAY AS WELL GO BIG AND STOCK UP FOR YOUR FUTURE SELF!

BE SURE THE DUMPLINGS ARE FULLY FROZEN BEFORE TRANSFERRING THEM TO A RESEALABLE FREEZER BAG. KEEP THAT BAG TIGHTLY SEALED TO PREVENT ANY FREEZER BURN.

FROZEN DUMPLINGS ARE BEST WHEN STEAMED OR BOILED — RESIDUAL ICE CAN CAUSE SOME DANGEROUS SPLATTERS WHEN PAN-FRYING OR DEEP-FRYING.

COOK FROZEN DUMPLINGS STRAIGHT FROM THE FREEZER —

DON'T THAW THEM FIRST, OR THEY WILL BECOME STICKY AND MESSY AND GENERALLY IMPOSSIBLE TO WORK WITH —

AND BE SURE TO ADD 3 TO 5 MINUTES OF EXTRA COOKING TIME.

BAOZI ARE BEST PROOFED AND COOKED FRESH, SO WE DON'T RECOMMEND FREEZING THEM!

LAY UNCOOKED DUMPLINGS IN A SINGLE LAYER ON A PARCHMENT PAPER—LINED SHEET PAN, MAKING SURE THEY DON'T TOUCH.

PLACE UNCOVERED IN THE FREEZER UNTIL COMPLETELY FROZEN THROUGH, AT LEAST OVERNIGHT.

ONCE FROZEN, GENTLY TRANSFER THE DUMPLINGS TO A RESEALABLE FREEZER BAG,

BOIL (P. 50) OR STEAM (P. 52).

SEAL TIGHTLY, AND KEEP FROZEN FOR UP TO 2 MONTHS.

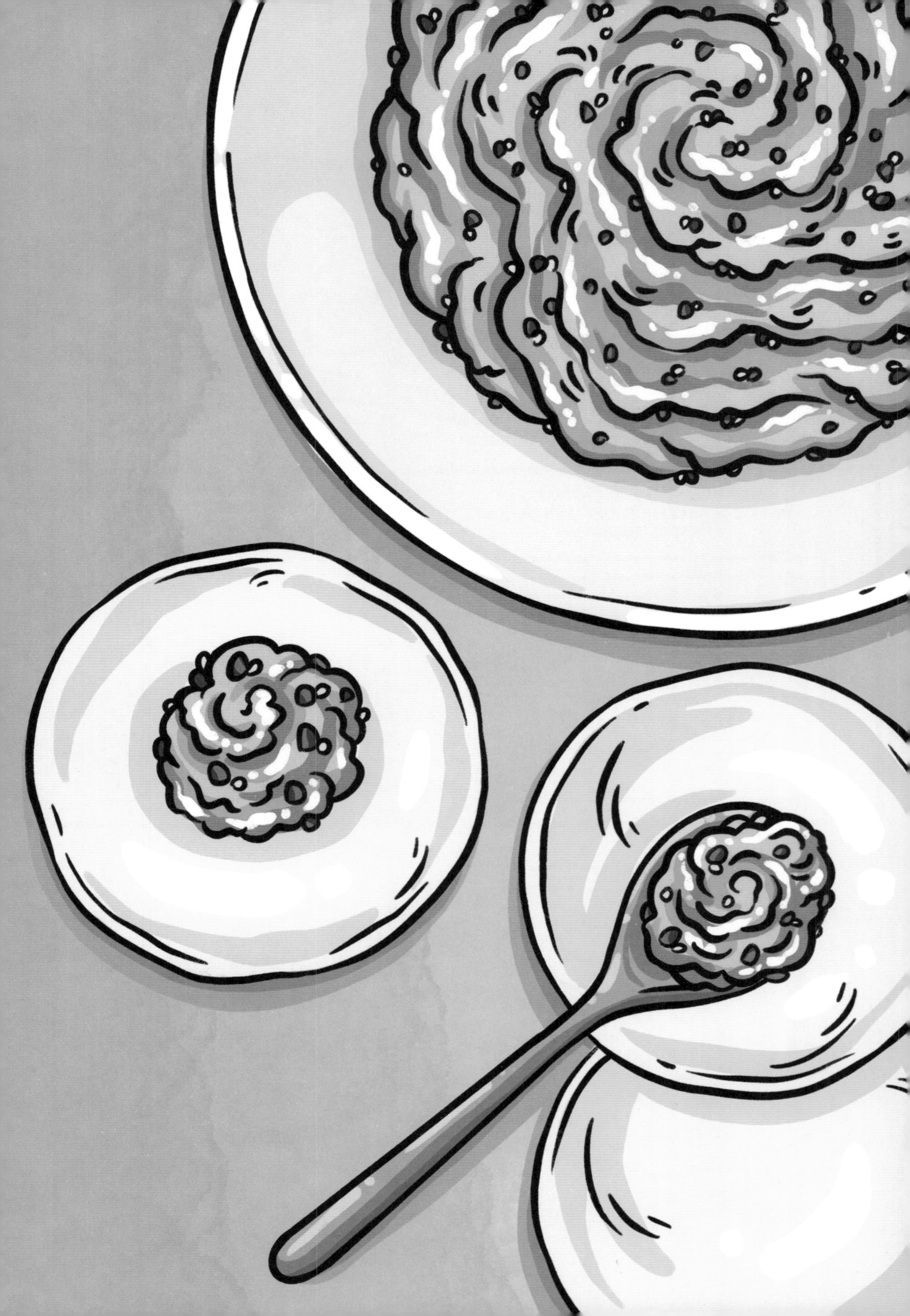

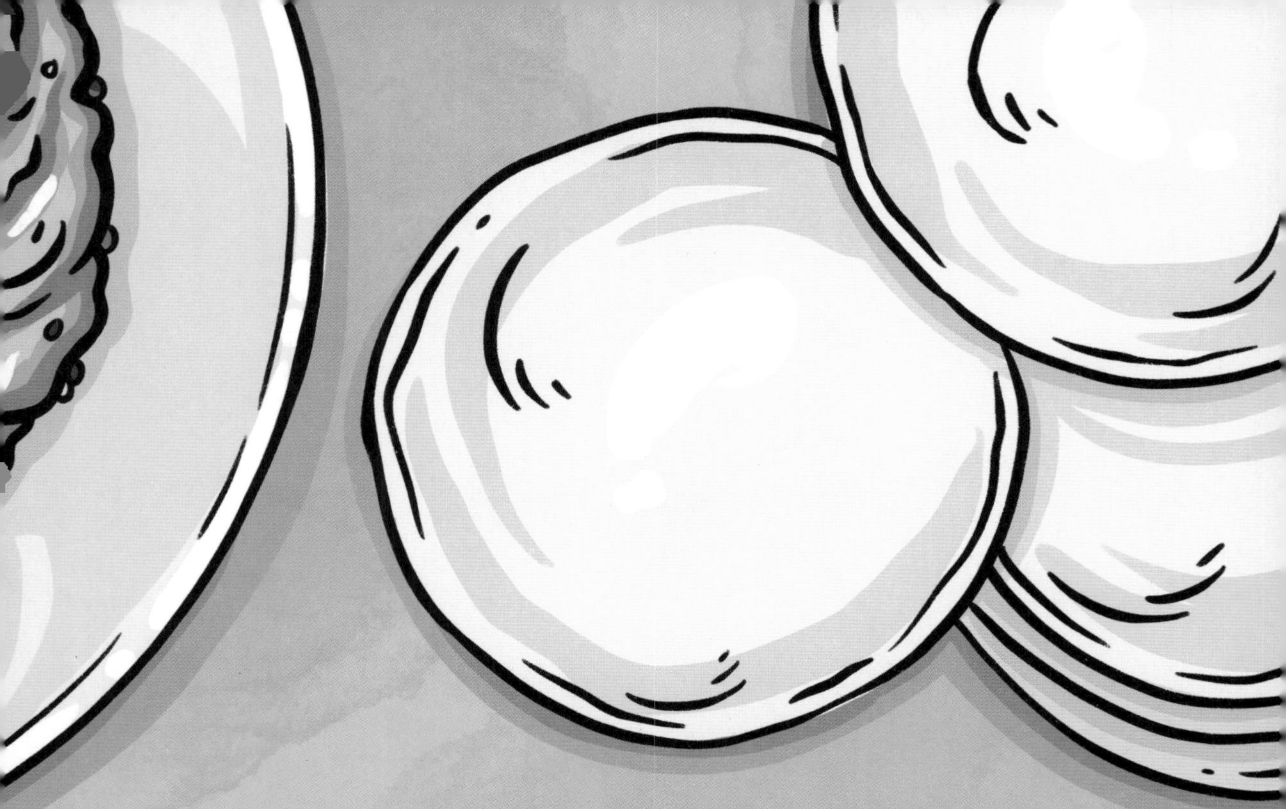

RECIPES

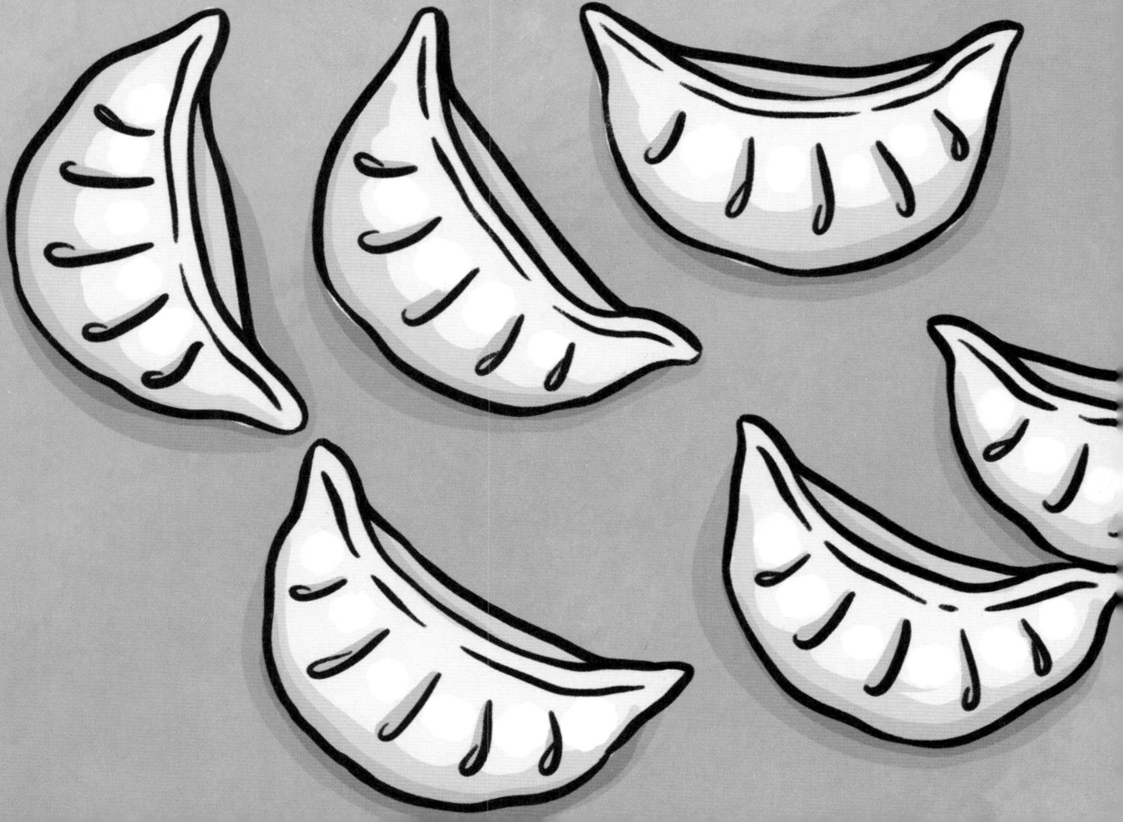

a word about MAKING & EATING DUMPLINGS

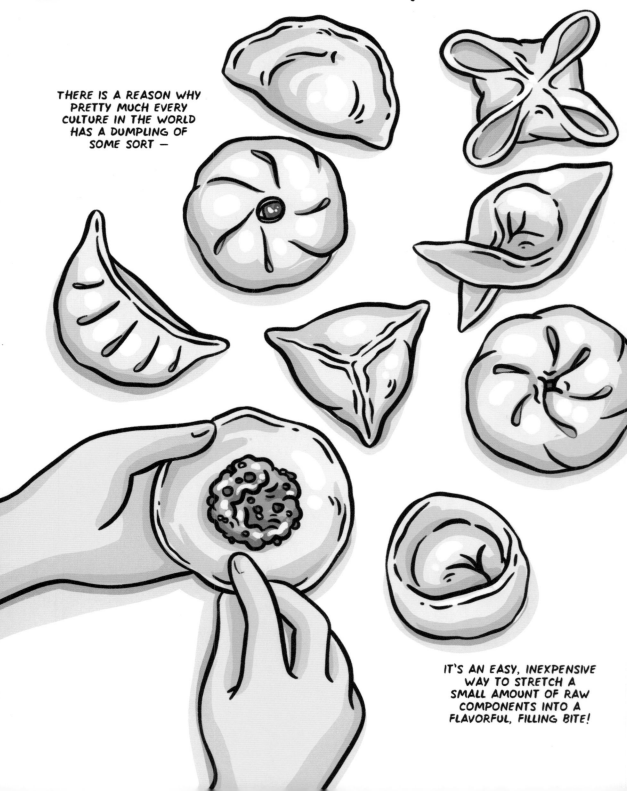

THERE IS A REASON WHY PRETTY MUCH EVERY CULTURE IN THE WORLD HAS A DUMPLING OF SOME SORT —

IT'S AN EASY, INEXPENSIVE WAY TO STRETCH A SMALL AMOUNT OF RAW COMPONENTS INTO A FLAVORFUL, FILLING BITE!

FOLLOW THE BASIC BLUEPRINT OF WRAPPING TASTY INGREDIENTS INSIDE A DUMPLING OR WONTON WRAPPER

AND COOK IT AS DIRECTED IN THE COOKING DUMPLINGS GUIDE (P. 47).

YOU'LL FIND SUCCESS MORE TIMES THAN NOT!

LIKEWISE, THERE'S NO WAY TO GO WRONG EATING A DUMPLING —

THE STANDARD METHOD IS TO USE GENTLE PRESSURE ON ITS PLUMP SIDES TO PICK IT UP WITH CHOPSTICKS

AND DIP IT IN SAUCE BEFORE TAKING A BITE

(DOUBLE DIPPING IS TOTALLY UP TO YOU AND YOUR DUMPLING-EATING CREW!).

IF IT'S TOO SLIPPERY, GO AHEAD AND SKEWER IT WITH YOUR CHOPSTICKS — THERE ARE WORSE THINGS THAT COULD BE DONE.

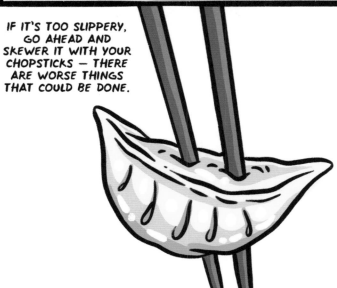

AND AT THE END OF THE DAY, IF YOU HAVE TO JUST PICK IT UP WITH YOUR BARE HANDS, BY ALL MEANS, DO SO!

ONE NOTE: XIAOLONGBAO (P. 83) ARE A BIT UNIQUE SINCE THEY ARE SOUP DUMPLINGS FILLED WITH WARM BROTH,

SO CAREFULLY PICK ONE UP, REST IT ON YOUR SPOON, AND GIVE IT A LITTLE NIBBLE ON THE TOP CORNER TO EXPOSE THE STEAMING SOUP INSIDE.

BLOW ON THE DUMPLING GENTLY TO COOL,

TIP IT INTO YOUR MOUTH, AND SLURP THE SOUP OUT

BEFORE CHOMPING THE REST OF THE DUMPLING DOWN.

IT'LL ALL COME NATURALLY — AND PRACTICING HAS NEVER BEEN MORE DELICIOUS!

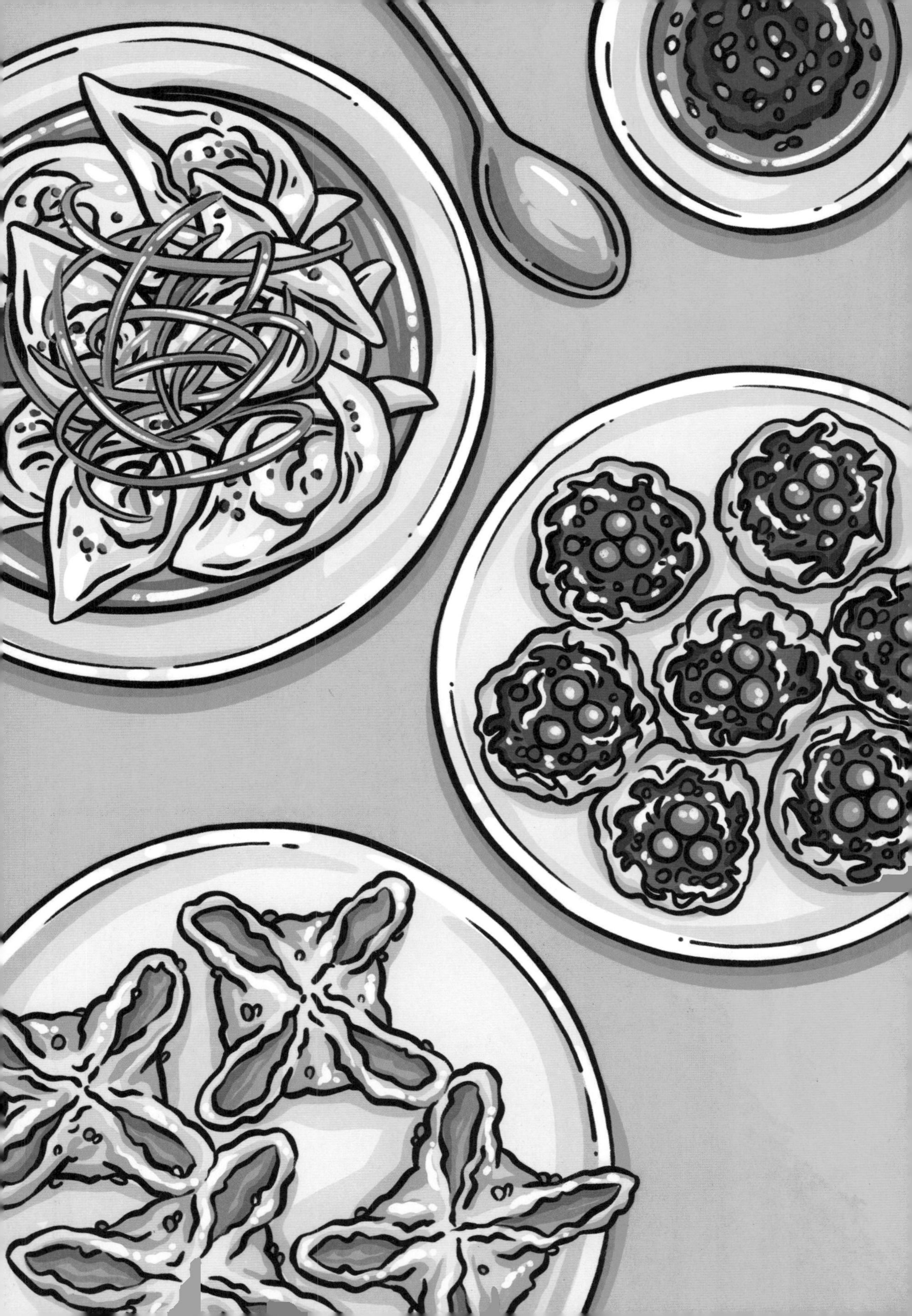

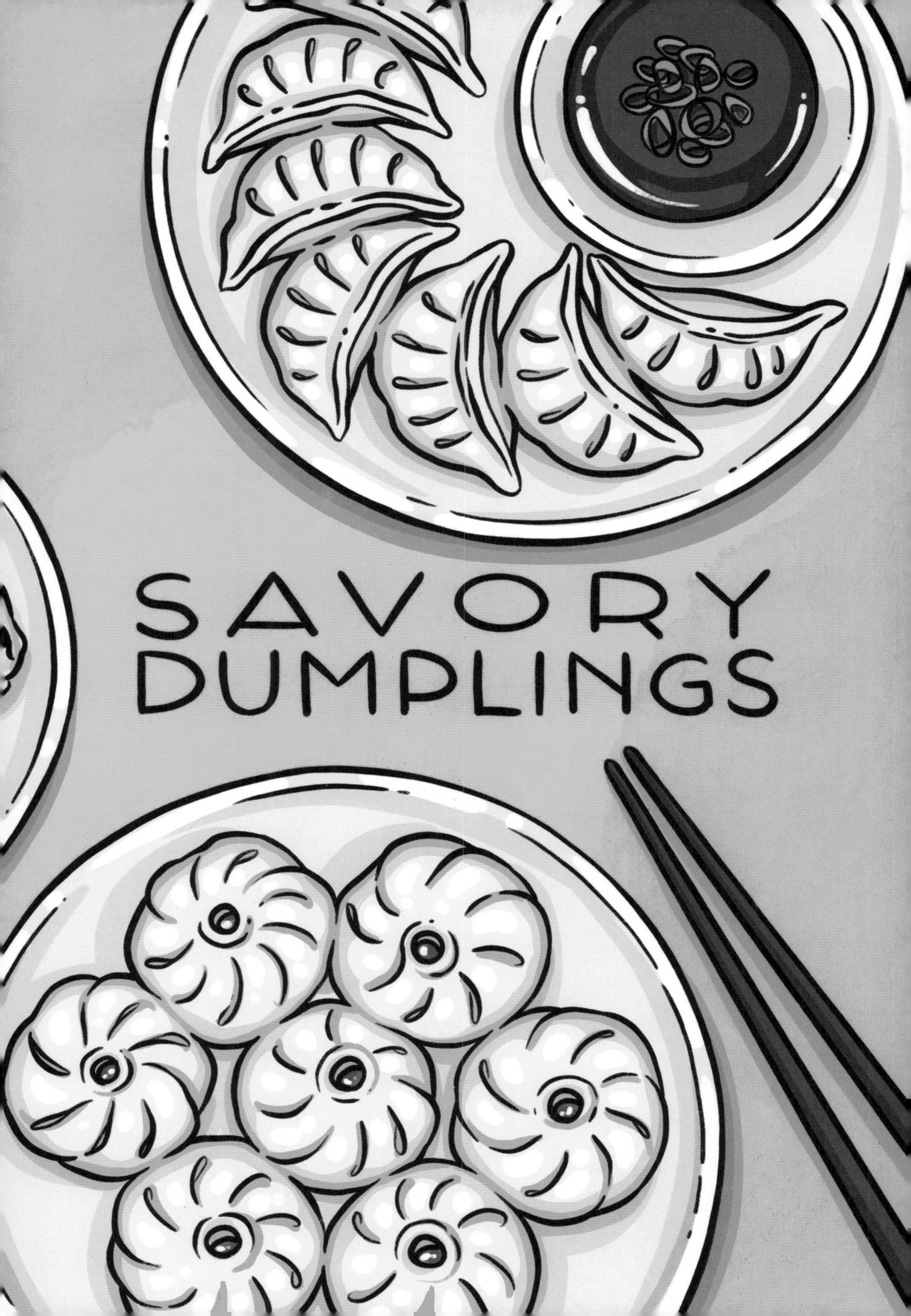
SAVORY
DUMPLINGS

a word about GYOZA

SUPER NOSTALGIC FOR US, AND LOVE AT FIRST BITE FOR THE NEWLY INITIATED, GYOZA ARE JAPAN'S DESCENDANT OF CHINESE JIAOZI (P. 78).

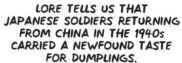

LORE TELLS US THAT JAPANESE SOLDIERS RETURNING FROM CHINA IN THE 1940s CARRIED A NEWFOUND TASTE FOR DUMPLINGS.

WHEAT IMPORTED DURING THE LEAN PERIOD OF THE AMERICAN OCCUPATION PROVED TO BE AN IMPORTANT FOOD SOURCE, ALLOWING TWO CLASSICS OF JAPANESE WORKING-CLASS FOOD TO BLOSSOM: RAMEN AND GYOZA.

FILLED WITH GARLIC (THOUGHT TO PROVIDE STAMINA) AND PORK,

GYOZA WAS AN INEXPENSIVE, EASY-TO-EAT FOOD HIGH IN CALORIES AND LOW IN COST.

SERVED FROM YATAIS (JAPANESE STREET CART VENDORS), IT BECAME AN INSTANT CLASSIC,

ESPECIALLY NORTH OF TOKYO IN UTSUNOMIYA, HOME TO MANY OF THE RETURNING SOLDIERS, NOW A GLOBAL CAPITAL OF GYOZA SHOPS.

MAKE THESE IN BULK — THEY FREEZE BEAUTIFULLY —

AND GRAB A COLD BEER; WE COULD EAT GYOZA AND DRINK BEER ALL NIGHT!

GYOZA

INGREDIENTS:

½ MEDIUM CABBAGE, CORE REMOVED, LEAVES FINELY MINCED (ABOUT 3½ CUPS MINCED AND LIGHTLY PACKED)

2 TEASPOONS SALT

1 POUND GROUND PORK

1 BUNCH GREEN ONIONS, TRIMMED AND MINCED

6 GARLIC CLOVES, MINCED

3-INCH PIECE GINGER, PEELED AND MINCED

1 TEASPOON FRESHLY GROUND BLACK PEPPER

1 TEASPOON SUGAR

2 TABLESPOONS SOY SAUCE

1 TABLESPOON TOASTED SESAME OIL

48 STORE-BOUGHT GYOZA WRAPPERS OR DUMPLING WRAPPERS (P. 27)

TOSS THE CABBAGE WITH THE SALT,

TRANSFER TO A FINE-MESH STRAINER, AND LET DRAIN FOR 30 MINUTES.

RAMEN-READY KITCHENS CAN USE A NOODLE BASKET!

A FOOD PROCESSOR MAKES SHORT WORK OF THE MINCING IN THIS RECIPE —

FOR BEST RESULTS, JUST BE SURE TO HELP THE MACHINE OUT BY COARSELY CUTTING THE CABBAGE INTO 1-INCH CHUNKS,

THE GREEN ONIONS INTO ¼-INCH PIECES,

AND THE GINGER INTO THIN SLICES ACROSS THE GRAIN.

PLACE THE CABBAGE ON A CLEAN DISH TOWEL,

BRING THE TOWEL'S CORNERS TOGETHER,

AND TWIST TO SQUEEZE OUT EXCESS MOISTURE.

IT'S VERY IMPORTANT TO REMOVE AS MUCH EXCESS MOISTURE AS POSSIBLE FROM THE CABBAGE TO KEEP THE FILLING FROM GETTING WATERY —

YOU SHOULD REMOVE ABOUT 1 CUP OF WATER FROM THE CABBAGE!

TRANSFER CABBAGE TO A LARGE BOWL

AND ADD THE PORK, GREEN ONIONS, GARLIC, GINGER, BLACK PEPPER, SUGAR, SOY SAUCE, AND SESAME OIL.

USE YOUR HAND TO VIGOROUSLY MIX THE FILLING UNTIL IT STARTS TO COME TOGETHER, 20 TO 30 SECONDS.

THEN "KNEAD" THE FILLING BY FOLDING IT OVER ON ITSELF REPEATEDLY FOR ANOTHER 90 SECONDS.

FINISH EMULSIFYING THE FILLING BY CONTINUOUSLY PICKING IT UP

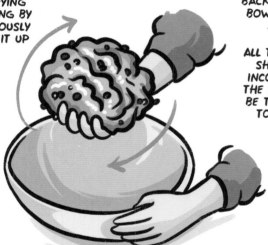

AND SLAPPING IT BACK DOWN INTO THE BOWL FOR ANOTHER 30 SECONDS.

ALL THE INGREDIENTS SHOULD BE FULLY INCORPORATED AND THE MIXTURE SHOULD BE TACKY AND STICK TO YOUR HANDS.

YOU CAN ALSO USE A STANDING MIXER WITH A PADDLE ATTACHMENT TO EMULSIFY THE FILLING.

MIX ON MEDIUM-HIGH SPEED UNTIL THE SAME RESULTS ARE PRODUCED, ABOUT 1 MINUTE.

TO TRY THE FILLING, MICROWAVE A TEASPOON OF IT FOR 20 TO 30 SECONDS

AND ADJUST SEASONING TO TASTE.

GYOZA ACTUALLY WORK BEST WITH THIN STORE-BOUGHT WRAPPERS, BUT IF USING HOMEMADE DUMPLING WRAPPERS (P. 27), BE SURE TO ROLL THEM EXTRA THIN!

FOLD!

FILL EACH WRAPPER WITH ABOUT 2 TEASPOONS OF FILLING AND SHAPE AS DESIRED (WE RECOMMEND THE PLEATED CRESCENT, P. 36).

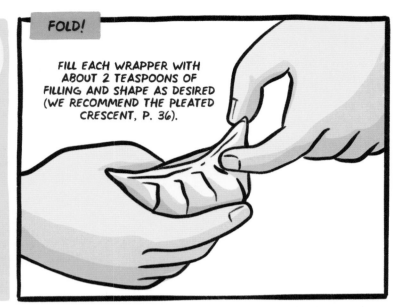

COOK!

COOK AS DESIRED (WE LIKE PAN-FRYING, P. 56, AND DEEP FRYING, P. 59)

WE LOVE THESE PAN-FRIED AS JAPANESE POTSTICKERS, BUT THEY'RE ALSO GREAT WHEN DEEP-FRIED AND CRUNCHY!

SERVE!

AND SERVE WITH GYOZA SAUCE (P. 183) OR RAYU-KEWPIE MAYONNAISE (P. 184).

ALTERNATIVELY, FREEZE UNCOOKED (P. 62).

a word about JIAOZI

JIAOZI ARE CHINESE DUMPLINGS THAT CAN BE FILLED WITH NEARLY ANYTHING,

AND THEY ARE THE ORIGINAL DUMPLING FROM WHICH JAPANESE GYOZA (P. 74) EVOLVED.

THIS PARTICULAR FILLING IS GREAT FOR COOL AUTUMN NIGHTS, WHEN THOUGHTS WANDER FONDLY TO WARM KITCHEN HEARTHS AND PANTRIES FILLED WITH FALL SQUASHES.

GRATED RAW BUTTERNUT SQUASH STEAMS INSIDE THE DUMPLING,

SWEETENING THE PORK AND MAKING FOR A DELICIOUS COLD-WEATHER DUMPLING.

USE THE LARGE HOLES ON A BOX GRATER TO GRATE THE SQUASH, AND BE VERY CAREFUL AS THE SQUASH CAN BE SLIPPERY!

BUTTERNUT PORK JIAOZI

INGREDIENTS:

2 CUPS PEELED, SEEDED, AND GRATED BUTTERNUT SQUASH (ABOUT ½ LARGE SQUASH), LIGHTLY PACKED

2 TEASPOONS SALT

12 OUNCES GROUND PORK

3 GREEN ONIONS, TRIMMED AND MINCED

3 GARLIC CLOVES, MINCED

2-INCH PIECE GINGER, PEELED AND MINCED

1 LARGE EGG

1 TEASPOON FRESHLY GROUND BLACK PEPPER

1 TABLESPOON SOY SAUCE

1 TEASPOON RICE VINEGAR

36–48 STORE-BOUGHT GYOZA WRAPPERS OR DUMPLING WRAPPERS (P. 27)

TOSS THE SQUASH WITH 1 TEASPOON OF THE SALT,

TRANSFER TO A FINE-MESH STRAINER, AND LET DRAIN FOR 30 MINUTES.

SQUEEZE OUT AS MUCH LIQUID AS POSSIBLE (THERE WILL BE JUST A FEW TABLESPOONS)

AND TRANSFER THE SQUASH TO A LARGE BOWL.

ADD THE PORK, GREEN ONIONS, GARLIC, GINGER, EGG, BLACK PEPPER, SOY SAUCE, VINEGAR, AND REMAINING 1 TEASPOON SALT.

USE YOUR HAND TO VIGOROUSLY MIX THE FILLING UNTIL IT STARTS TO COME TOGETHER, 20 TO 30 SECONDS.

THEN "KNEAD" THE FILLING BY FOLDING IT OVER ON ITSELF REPEATEDLY FOR ANOTHER 90 SECONDS.

FINISH EMULSIFYING THE FILLING BY CONTINUOUSLY PICKING IT UP

AND SLAPPING IT BACK DOWN IN THE BOWL FOR ANOTHER 30 SECONDS.

TO TRY THE FILLING, MICROWAVE ABOUT A TEASPOON OF IT FOR 20 TO 30 SECONDS AND ADJUST THE SEASONING TO TASTE.

THE MIXTURE SHOULD BE COHESIVE.

FOLD!

FILL EACH WRAPPER WITH ABOUT 2 TEASPOONS OF FILLING AND FOLD AS DESIRED (WE RECOMMEND THE HALF-MOON, P. 34, OR THE PLEATED CRESCENT, P. 36).

COOK!

COOK AS DESIRED (WE LIKE BOILING, P. 50)

SERVE!

AND SERVE WITH A DESIRED SAUCE (WE RECOMMEND BLACK VINEGAR DIPPING SAUCE, P. 182, OR FRIED GARLIC OIL, P. 194).

ALTERNATIVELY, FREEZE UNCOOKED (P. 62).

a word about XIAOLONGBAO

THESE MAGICAL
DUMPLINGS ARE KNOWN
AS "SOUP DUMPLINGS"
DUE TO THE DELICIOUS
BROTH THAT IS SEALED
INSIDE THE WRAPPER.

XIAOLONGBAO
ARE ACTUALLY PRETTY
SIMPLE TO MAKE —
THEY JUST REQUIRE SOME
ADVANCE PLANNING.

THE FOUNDATION HERE IS MAKING A CONCENTRATED STOCK THE DAY BEFORE WRAPPING

SO THAT IT BECOMES A STIFF GELATIN WHEN COOLED AND CAN BE FOLDED INTO THE REST OF THE FILLING AS A SOLID.

WHEN COOKED, THE STOCK MELTS INTO A FLAVORFUL SOUP INSIDE THE WRAPPER.

MANY RECIPES FOR XIAOLONGBAO RECOMMEND FORTIFYING STORE-BOUGHT STOCKS WITH POWDERED GELATIN,

BUT WE LIKE TO MAKE THINGS FROM START TO FINISH,

SO THIS RECIPE STARTS WITH A COLLAGEN-FILLED STOCK MADE FROM CHICKEN BACKS AND WINGS FOR PLENTY OF GELATIN CONTENT.

REMEMBER, THE COLDER THE FILLING REMAINS, THE MORE SOLID THE GELATIN WILL BE, AND THUS THE EASIER THE DUMPLINGS WILL BE TO FOLD.

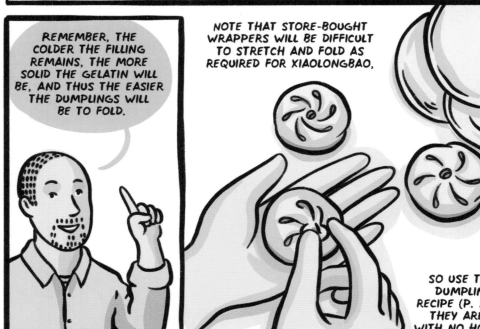

NOTE THAT STORE-BOUGHT WRAPPERS WILL BE DIFFICULT TO STRETCH AND FOLD AS REQUIRED FOR XIAOLONGBAO,

SO USE THE HOMEMADE DUMPLING WRAPPERS RECIPE (P. 27) AND BE SURE THEY ARE ARE SMOOTH WITH NO HOLES TO KEEP ALL THAT PRECIOUS SOUP INSIDE!

XIAOLONGBAO

INGREDIENTS:

8 OUNCES GROUND PORK

3 GREEN ONIONS, TRIMMED AND MINCED

1 TEASPOON SUGAR

1/4 TEASPOON GROUND WHITE PEPPER

2 TABLESPOONS SOY SAUCE

1 TABLESPOON SHAOXING WINE (SEE PANTRY, P. 19)

1 CUP CONCENTRATED AND CHILLED CHICKEN STOCK (P. 87)

24 DUMPLING WRAPPERS (P. 27)

PLACE PORK, GREEN ONIONS, SUGAR, WHITE PEPPER, SOY SAUCE, AND SHAOXING WINE IN A MEDIUM BOWL.

USE YOUR HAND TO VIGOROUSLY MIX UNTIL THOROUGHLY COMBINED, 20 TO 30 SECONDS.

THEN "KNEAD" THE FILLING BY FOLDING IT OVER ON ITSELF REPEATEDLY FOR ANOTHER 90 SECONDS.

FINISH EMULSIFYING THE FILLING BY CONTINUOUSLY PICKING IT UP

AND SLAPPING IT BACK DOWN INTO THE BOWL FOR ANOTHER 30 SECONDS.

TO TRY THE FILLING, MICROWAVE ABOUT A TEASPOON OF IT FOR 20 TO 30 SECONDS AND ADJUST SEASONING TO TASTE.

ADD THE CHILLED CHICKEN STOCK AND MIX WELL WITH A SPOON UNTIL WELL INCORPORATED.

USE A SPOON (RATHER THAN YOUR WARM HAND) TO MIX IN THE CHILLED STOCK TO KEEP THINGS AS COLD AS POSSIBLE!

COVER AND REFRIGERATE THE MIXTURE FOR AT LEAST 1 HOUR BEFORE FILLING THE WRAPPERS.

WORKING IN BATCHES TO KEEP THE FILLING AS COOL AS POSSIBLE,

START BY PLACING A THIRD OF THE FILLING IN A SMALL BOWL

AND KEEP THE REST REFRIGERATED UNTIL NEEDED.

FOLD!

FILL EACH WRAPPER WITH ABOUT 2 TEASPOONS OF FILLING AND SHAPE AS A MOMO (P. 42),

MAKING SURE TO GIVE THE TOP A PINCH TO GUARANTEE IT IS SEALED.

IT CAN BE HELPFUL TO REST THE DUMPLING ON A SURFACE WHILE FOLDING FOR MAXIMUM SUPPORT!

COOK!

COOK AS SHOWN UNDER STEAMING (P. 52)

SERVE!

AND SERVE IMMEDIATELY.

ALTERNATIVELY, FREEZE UNCOOKED (P. 62).

NO SAUCE IS NEEDED BECAUSE OF THE DELICIOUS SOUP FORMED INSIDE THE DUMPLING,

BUT IF YOU LIKE, YOU CAN SERVE WITH A BIT OF BLACK VINEGAR (SEE PANTRY, P. 18) MIXED WITH MINCED GINGER.

a word about CHICKEN STOCK

THIS IS A BASIC CHICKEN STOCK THAT WORKS GREAT FOR WONTON SOUP (P. 105) AS WELL AS FOR THE SOUP INSIDE XIAOLONGBAO (P. 83) AND SHENG JIAN BAOZI (P. 142) WHEN REDUCED.

NOTE THAT A GOAL IN THIS RECIPE IS TO PRODUCE A STOCK FULL OF GELATIN,

SO IT SHOULD SOLIDIFY WHEN COOLED AND HAVE A RICH MOUTHFEEL WHEN HOT.

IF USING FOR ANYTHING BUT XIAOLONGBAO OR SHENG JIAN BAOZI, OMIT THE SMOKY BACON.

CHICKEN STOCK

INGREDIENTS:

3 POUNDS CHICKEN BACKS OR WINGS

4 OUNCES SMOKY BACON (OPTIONAL; ONLY IF MAKING FOR USE IN XIAOLONGBAO, P. 83 OR SHENG JIAN BAOZI, P. 142)

1 BUNCH GREEN ONIONS, TRIMMED AND HALVED CROSSWISE

4 OUNCES GINGER, SLICED 1/4 INCH THICK

3 GARLIC CLOVES, PEELED

1 1/2 TEASPOONS SALT

4 QUARTS COLD WATER

PLACE ALL THE INGREDIENTS IN A LARGE POT AND BRING TO A SIMMER OVER MEDIUM-HIGH HEAT.

CHICKEN BACKS AND WINGS HAVE A HIGH COLLAGEN CONTENT THAT WILL COOK DOWN INTO GELATIN, CRUCIAL FOR SNEAKING THE SOUP INTO XIAOLONGBAO!

LOWER THE HEAT TO MAINTAIN A SLOW SIMMER.

COOK FOR 3 HOURS, SKIMMING OFF ANY SCUM THAT RISES TO THE SURFACE OF THE LIQUID

AND AGITATING THE CHICKEN BONES EVERY HALF HOUR OR SO.

THE STOCK WILL REDUCE TO ABOUT 2 QUARTS DURING THE COOKING PROCESS — THIS IS NORMAL.

REMOVE FROM THE HEAT AND LET COOL TO ROOM TEMPERATURE.

STRAIN, PICKING ANY REMAINING MEAT FROM THE BONES AND RESERVING FOR ANOTHER USE.

DISCARD ALL OTHER SOLIDS.

IF USING FOR XIAOLONGBAO (P. 83) OR SHENG JIAN BAOZI (P. 142), RETURN THE STOCK TO A POT

AND SIMMER OVER MEDIUM-HIGH HEAT UNTIL THE GELATIN CONTENT HAS CONCENTRATED AND THE STOCK HAS REDUCED TO ABOUT 1 QUART.

REFRIGERATE THE STOCK OVERNIGHT, TIGHTLY COVERED.

THE NEXT DAY, REMOVE THE CONGEALED FAT FROM THE TOP OF THE STOCK AND REFRIGERATE FOR ANOTHER USE, UP TO 1 MONTH.

REFRIGERATE THE STOCK UNTIL YOU'RE READY TO USE IT, UP TO 1 WEEK, OR FREEZE FOR UP TO 6 MONTHS.

a word about MANDU

MANDU IS THE KOREAN STANDARD FOR DUMPLINGS,

AND AS WITH JAPANESE GYOZA (P. 74) AND CHINESE JIAOZI (P. 79), THEY CAN BE FILLED WITH PRETTY MUCH ANYTHING DELICIOUS AND SAVORY.

WE LIKE TO FILL OURS WITH FORCEFULLY FUNKY AND FIERY KIMCHI, BEEF, AND PLENTY OF GOCHUJANG — THE KOREAN FERMENTED CHILE PASTE.

FIND GOCHUJANG IN ASIAN MARKETS OR ONLINE!

GOT A COLD, SNOWY DAY ON YOUR HANDS? WARM UP WITH THESE MANDU SWIMMING IN A STEAMY BOWL OF MANDU GUK (P. 92)!

BEEF & KIMCHI MANDU

MAKES 36-48 MANDU

INGREDIENTS:

1 POUND GROUND BEEF

1 CUP KIMCHI, FINELY CHOPPED AND LIGHTLY SQUEEZED TO REMOVE EXCESS LIQUID

1 BUNCH GREEN ONIONS, TRIMMED AND MINCED

3 GARLIC CLOVES, MINCED

2-INCH PIECE GINGER, PEELED AND MINCED

1 LARGE EGG

1½ TEASPOONS SALT

1 TEASPOON SUGAR

3 TABLESPOONS GOCHUJANG

1 TABLESPOON TOASTED SESAME OIL

1 TEASPOON RICE VINEGAR

36-48 ROUND STORE-BOUGHT GYOZA WRAPPERS OR DUMPLING WRAPPERS (P. 27)

PLACE BEEF, KIMCHI, GREEN ONIONS, GARLIC, GINGER, EGG, SALT, SUGAR, GOCHUJANG, SESAME OIL, AND VINEGAR IN A LARGE BOWL.

USE YOUR HAND TO VIGOROUSLY MIX THE FILLING UNTIL ALL INGREDIENTS ARE INCORPORATED, 20 TO 30 SECONDS.

THEN "KNEAD" THE FILLING BY FOLDING IT OVER ON ITSELF REPEATEDLY FOR ANOTHER 90 SECONDS.

THE MIXTURE SHOULD BE COHESIVE

AND WON'T NEED THE FORCEFUL SLAPPING MOTION USED IN THE WETTER PORK-BASED FILLINGS.

TO TRY THE FILLING, MICROWAVE ABOUT A TEASPOON OF IT FOR 20 TO 30 SECONDS

AND ADJUST THE SEASONING TO TASTE.

FOLD!

FILL EACH WRAPPER WITH ABOUT 2 TEASPOONS OF FILLING AND FOLD AS DESIRED

(IF DEEP-FRYING OR PAN-FRYING, WE RECOMMEND THE HALF-MOON, P. 34, OR PLEATED CRESCENT, P. 36).

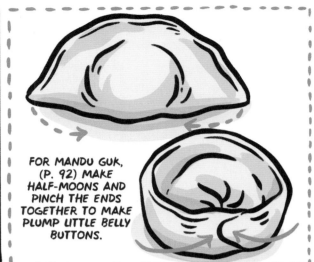

FOR MANDU GUK, (P. 92) MAKE HALF-MOONS AND PINCH THE ENDS TOGETHER TO MAKE PLUMP LITTLE BELLY BUTTONS.

COOK!

COOK AS DESIRED (WE LIKE PAN-FRYING, P. 56, AND DEEP-FRYING, P. 59)

SERVE!

AND SERVE WITHOUT ANY SAUCE (THESE ARE BURSTING WITH FLAVOR AND DON'T NECESSARILY NEED ONE)

OR SPICE IT UP A BIT WITH A LITTLE RAYU (P. 190).

YOU CAN ALSO SIMMER IN BROTH AS DIRECTED FOR MANDU GUK (P. 92), OR FREEZE UNCOOKED (P. 62).

MANDU GUK

KOREAN DUMPLING SOUP

INGREDIENTS:

1 POUND FLANK STEAK, WHOLE

1 ONION, QUARTERED

1 BUNCH GREEN ONIONS, TRIMMED; 2 THINLY SLICED DIAGONALLY, THE REMAINDER HALVED CROSSWISE

5 GARLIC CLOVES, SMASHED

4-INCH PIECE GINGER, PEELED AND SLICED 1/4 INCH THICK

1 TABLESPOON WHOLE BLACK PEPPERCORNS

2 TEASPOONS SALT, PLUS MORE AS NEEDED

12 CUPS COLD WATER

3 TABLESPOONS FISH SAUCE (SEE PANTRY, P. 18)

1 TEASPOON TOASTED SESAME OIL

1/2 TEASPOON RICE VINEGAR

4 EGGS

1 TABLESPOON NEUTRAL OIL

20 BEEF & KIMCHI MANDU (P. 90), SHAPED FOR MANDU GUK

PUT THE WHOLE STEAK, ONION, HALVED GREEN ONIONS, GARLIC, GINGER, PEPPERCORNS, SALT, AND WATER INTO A LARGE POT.

BRING TO A BOIL OVER HIGH HEAT, THEN LOWER THE HEAT AND SIMMER, UNCOVERED, FOR 45 MINUTES.

THIS DUMPLING SOUP IS OFTEN MADE USING A LABOR-INTENSIVE BEEF AND ANCHOVY STOCK —

WE'VE SIMPLIFIED IT BY MAKING A DELICIOUSLY LIGHT BEEF BROTH USING FLANK STEAK, FISH SAUCE, AND PLENTY OF AROMATICS.

REMOVE FROM THE HEAT AND LET STAND FOR 15 MINUTES.

REMOVE THE FLANK STEAK FROM THE POT AND SET ASIDE; STRAIN THE SOUP AND DISCARD ALL THE OTHER SOLIDS.

YOU SHOULD HAVE ABOUT 8 CUPS OF BROTH.

ADD THE FISH SAUCE, SESAME OIL, AND VINEGAR TO THE BROTH AND TASTE, ADJUSTING THE SEASONING WITH ADDITIONAL SALT IF NECESSARY.

RETURN THE SOUP TO THE POT AND SIMMER OVER LOW HEAT AS YOU PREPARE THE EGG TOPPING.

NOTE THAT EGG IS BOTH SWIRLED INTO THE HOT BROTH A LA EGG DROP SOUP

HEAT A MEDIUM NONSTICK SKILLET OVER MEDIUM HEAT WHILE YOU BEAT 2 OF THE EGGS WITH A PINCH OF SALT.

AND COOKED AND SLICED AS A GARNISH.

ADD THE NEUTRAL OIL TO THE PAN AND SWIRL,

THEN ADD THE EGGS AND LET THEM SPREAD ACROSS THE PAN'S SURFACE.

COOK FOR 1 MINUTE, THEN FLIP.

REMOVE FROM THE HEAT AND LET SIT UNTIL SET, ABOUT 1 MINUTE.

TRANSFER TO A CUTTING BOARD AND ROLL THE EGG ONTO ITSELF ONCE OR TWICE,

THEN SLICE IT IN ¼-INCH STRIPS AND SET ASIDE.

SLICE THE FLANK STEAK ACROSS THE GRAIN INTO ¼-INCH STRIPS AND SET ASIDE.

INCREASE THE HEAT FOR THE BROTH TO HIGH

AND ADD THE MANDU.

LET SIMMER UNTIL ALMOST COOKED THROUGH, 2 TO 3 MINUTES.

MEANWHILE, BEAT THE REMAINING 2 EGGS

AND DRIZZLE INTO THE SIMMERING STOCK.

REMOVE FROM THE HEAT AND LADLE THE SOUP AND FIVE DUMPLINGS INTO EACH OF FOUR BOWLS.

GARNISH WITH SLICED EGG, STEAK, AND DIAGONALLY CUT GREEN ONIONS

AND SERVE IMMEDIATELY.

a word about POTSTICKERS

THE TERM "POTSTICKER" REFERS MORE TO A TECHNIQUE THAN A SPECIFIC DUMPLING —

START WITH PAN-FRYING A DUMPLING, THEN ADD WATER AND COVER THE PAN TO FINISH COOKING THE DUMPLINGS THROUGH WITH STEAM,

CREATING A DELIGHTFULLY GOLDEN BROWN AND CRISPY CRUST ON THE BOTTOM; A SOFT, CHEWY TOP; AND A PERFECTLY COOKED FILLING INSIDE.

SEE PAN-FRYING DUMPLINGS (P. 56) FOR SPECIFIC COOKING INSTRUCTIONS!

LEGEND HAS IT THAT A FORGETFUL COOK LEFT THE DUMPLINGS FRYING TOO LONG.

IN A PANIC, HE THREW WATER IN THE PAN

AND BY THE TIME EVERYTHING HAD SETTLED DOWN, HE HAD NO CHOICE BUT TO SERVE THE DUMPLINGS.

OF COURSE THEY WERE DELICIOUS, AND THE COOK TOOK THE CREDIT AS THOUGH HE'D DONE IT INTENTIONALLY!

THESE ARE OFTEN CALLED GUOTIE IN CHINESE —

"GUO" IS MANDARIN FOR WOK, AND "TIE" DESCRIBES SOMETHING ADHERED OR STUCK TO SOMETHING ELSE.

BUT DON'T WORRY — WHEN COOKED CORRECTLY, THEY WILL LIFT FREE FROM THE PAN WITH NO PROBLEM.

PORK AND CHIVES IS A POPULAR FILLING FOR CHINESE DUMPLINGS —

YOU CAN USE STANDARD CHIVES, BUT IF YOU CAN FIND FLAT CHINESE GARLIC CHIVES, ALL THE BETTER.

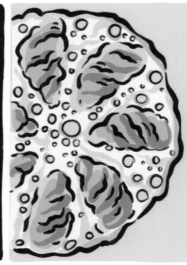

ADD A SIMPLE MIXTURE OF FLOUR AND WATER DURING THE PAN-FRYING PROCESS TO TAKE YOUR POTSTICKERS TO THE NEXT LEVEL WITH A DELICATELY CRISP AND LACY CREPE UPGRADE!

PORK & CHIVE POTSTICKERS

MAKES ABOUT 48 POTSTICKERS

INGREDIENTS:

1 POUND GROUND PORK

½ CUP MINCED GARLIC CHIVES (ABOUT 1 BUNCH), OR ½ CUP MINCED CHIVES AND 2 GARLIC CLOVES, MINCED

3-INCH PIECE GINGER, PEELED AND MINCED

1 TEASPOON SALT

½ TEASPOON SUGAR

½ TEASPOON GROUND WHITE PEPPER

2 TABLESPOONS SOY SAUCE

1 TEASPOON TOASTED SESAME OIL

½ TEASPOON RICE VINEGAR

48 STORE-BOUGHT GYOZA WRAPPERS OR DUMPLING WRAPPERS (P. 27)

PLACE THE PORK, CHIVES, GINGER, SALT, SUGAR, WHITE PEPPER, SOY SAUCE, SESAME OIL, AND VINEGAR IN A MEDIUM BOWL.

THEN "KNEAD" THE FILLING BY FOLDING IT OVER ON ITSELF REPEATEDLY FOR ANOTHER 90 SECONDS.

USE YOUR HAND TO VIGOROUSLY MIX THE FILLING UNTIL IT STARTS TO COME TOGETHER, 20 TO 30 SECONDS.

FINISH EMULSIFYING THE FILLING BY CONTINUOUSLY PICKING IT UP AND SLAPPING IT BACK DOWN INTO THE BOWL FOR ANOTHER 30 SECONDS.

THE MIXTURE SHOULD BE COHESIVE AND STICKY.

TO TRY THE FILLING, MICROWAVE ABOUT A TEASPOON OF IT FOR 20 TO 30 SECONDS AND ADJUST THE SEASONING TO TASTE.

FOLD!

FILL EACH WRAPPER WITH ABOUT 2 TEASPOONS OF FILLING EACH AND FOLD AS DESIRED (WE RECOMMEND THE HALF-MOON, P. 34, OR PLEATED CRESCENT, P. 36).

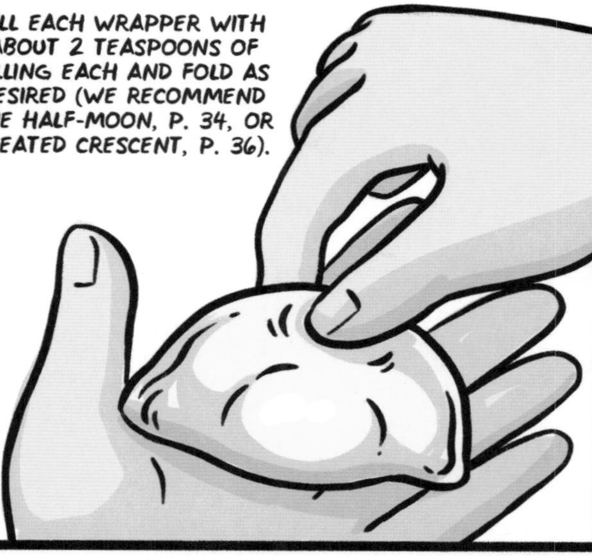

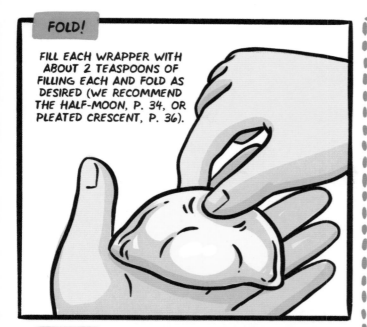

COOK!

COOK AS DIRECTED UNDER PAN-FRYING (P. 56)

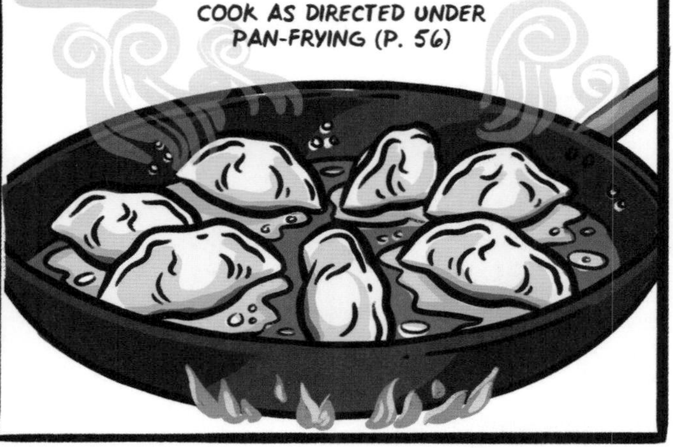

FOR THE LACY CREPE (SEE P. 97), BE SURE TO USE A NONSTICK PAN, AND SUBSTITUTE 1½ TEASPOONS FLOUR WHISKED WITH ½ CUP WATER FOR THE PLAIN WATER USED FOR PAN-FRYING.

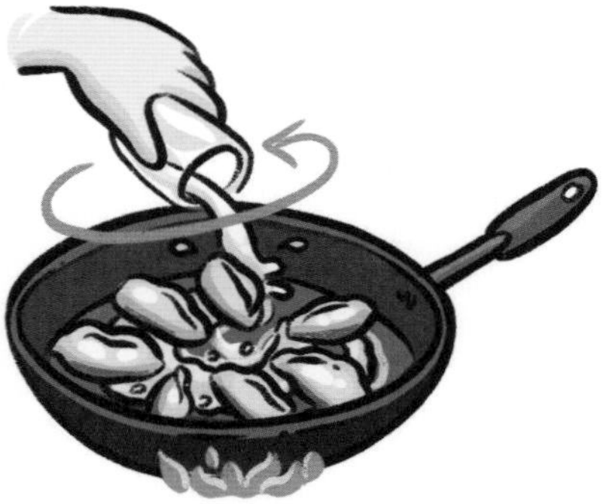

PROCEED AS DIRECTED, GENTLY BUT QUICKLY POURING THE SLURRY IN A CIRCULAR MOTION AROUND THE PAN WHEN THE WATER IS CALLED FOR. NOTE THAT THE MIXTURE WILL THIN OUT AS THE WATER EVAPORATES.

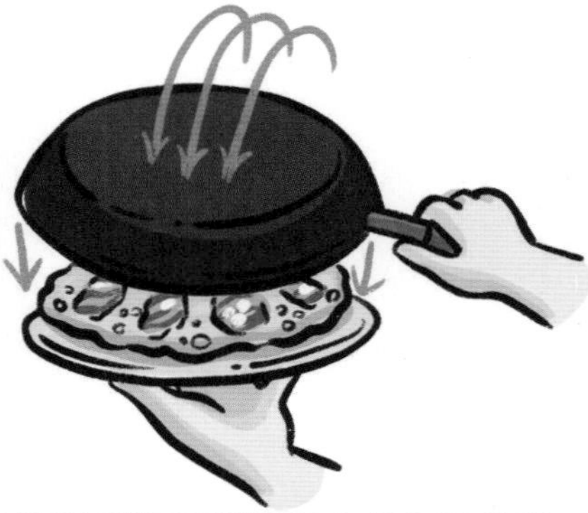

WHEN THE DUMPLINGS ARE COOKED THROUGH AND THE CREPE IS GOLDEN BROWN, CAREFULLY INVERT ONTO A PLATE SO THE LOVELY CREPE IS ON TOP!

SERVE!

AND SERVE WITH A SAUCE (WE LIKE BLACK VINEGAR DIPPING SAUCE, P. 182, OR GYOZA SAUCE, P. 183).

ALTERNATIVELY, FREEZE UNCOOKED (P. 62).

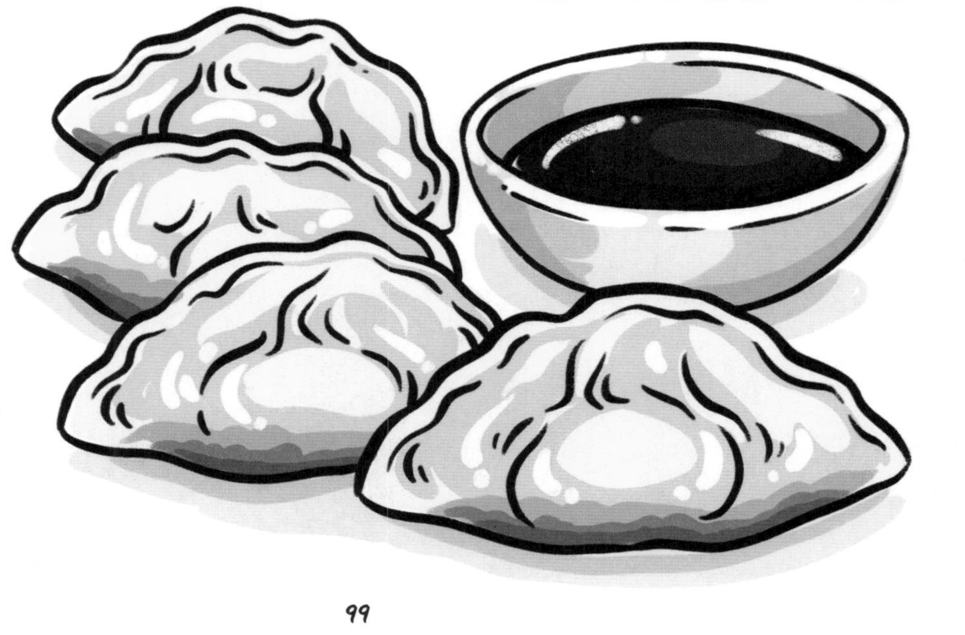

a word about WONTONS

WONTONS HAVE BEAUTIFUL CHINESE NAME ORIGINS, THE PHILOSOPHIES OF WHICH COULD FILL THEIR OWN BOOK:

IN MANDARIN, "HUNDUN" DESCRIBES THE CHAOS OF THE UNFORMED PRIMORDIAL UNIVERSE,

AND IN CANTONESE, "WANTAN" MEANS "SWALLOWING CLOUDS,"

PERHAPS MORE FAMILIAR TO THOSE ACCUSTOMED TO THESE DUMPLINGS FLOATING IN A LIGHTLY SEASONED BROTH.

WE'VE INCLUDED A RECIPE FOR WONTON SOUP (P. 105) IN THIS BOOK.

IF YOU PLAN TO MAKE THE SOUP, BUY FULLY INTACT SHRIMPS AND DO THE PEELING YOURSELF, RESERVING THE SHELLS (AND HEADS IF POSSIBLE) FOR THE BROTH.

AND PLEASE TRY A FAVORITE OF OURS — THE SPICY MA LA WONTONS (P. 103)!

WONTONS

MAKES ABOUT 50 WONTONS

INGREDIENTS:

8 OUNCES SHRIMP, PEELED AND DEVEINED

8 OUNCES GROUND PORK

2 GREEN ONIONS, TRIMMED AND MINCED

2-INCH PIECE GINGER, PEELED AND GRATED ON A MICROPLANE

1 EGG

1½ TEASPOONS SALT

1 TEASPOON SUGAR

1 TEASPOON FRESHLY GROUND BLACK PEPPER

2 TABLESPOONS SOY SAUCE

2 TEASPOONS TOASTED SESAME OIL

50 SQUARE STORE-BOUGHT OR HOMEMADE WONTON WRAPPERS (P. 31)

PLACE THE SHRIMP, GROUND PORK, GREEN ONIONS, GINGER, EGG, SALT, SUGAR, BLACK PEPPER, SOY SAUCE, AND SESAME OIL IN A FOOD PROCESSOR AND PULSE TWELVE TO FIFTEEN TIMES,

UNTIL THE SHRIMP IS BROKEN DOWN (BUT STILL SOMEWHAT CHUNKY) AND THE INGREDIENTS ARE THOROUGHLY COMBINED.

TRANSFER TO A MEDIUM BOWL AND MIX VIGOROUSLY WITH A LARGE SPOON UNTIL THE FILLING EMULSIFIES AND FEELS A BIT STIFFER, ABOUT 30 SECONDS.

TO TRY THE FILLING, MICROWAVE ABOUT A TEASPOON OF IT FOR 20 TO 30 SECONDS

AND ADJUST THE SEASONING TO TASTE.

THE FILLING CAN BE USED RIGHT AWAY OR REFRIGERATED FOR UP TO 3 DAYS IN AN AIRTIGHT CONTAINER.

FOLD!

FILL EACH WRAPPER WITH ABOUT 2 TEASPOONS OF FILLING, AND FOLD AS SHOWN FOR WONTONS IN FOLDING DUMPLINGS (P. 40).

NOTE THAT WONTON WRAPPERS ARE THINNER THAN OTHER DUMPLING WRAPPERS, SO BE SURE TO BUY WRAPPERS LABELED "WONTON WRAPPERS," OR PREFERABLY, FOLLOW OUR WONTON WRAPPER RECIPE (P. 31).

COOK!

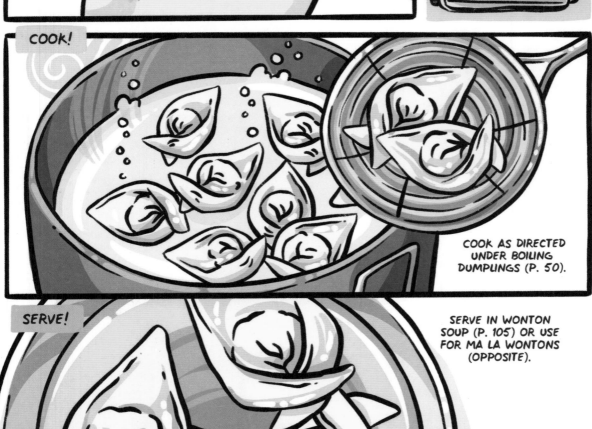

COOK AS DIRECTED UNDER BOILING DUMPLINGS (P. 50).

SERVE!

SERVE IN WONTON SOUP (P. 105) OR USE FOR MA LA WONTONS (OPPOSITE).

ALTERNATIVELY, FREEZE UNCOOKED (P. 62).

MA LA WONTONS

MAKES 12 WONTONS

INGREDIENTS:

½ TEASPOON SICHUAN PEPPERCORNS, OR MORE OR LESS TO TASTE

12 WONTONS (P. 101)

2 TO 4 TABLESPOONS RAYU (P. 190) OR OTHER CHILE OIL

1 GREEN ONION, TRIMMED AND THINLY SLICED ON THE DIAGONAL

1 TABLESPOON TOASTED WHITE SESAME SEEDS

GRIND THE PEPPERCORNS IN A SPICE GRINDER OR A MORTAR AND PESTLE

AND SIFT THROUGH A FINE-MESH STRAINER.

THESE WONTONS ARE INSPIRED BY SICHUAN STYLE MA (NUMBING) LA (SPICY) COOKING, WHICH USES PRODIGIOUS AMOUNTS OF SICHUAN PEPPERCORNS AND CHILES.

COOK THE WONTONS AS SUGGESTED UNDER BOILING DUMPLINGS (P. 50).

LOOK FOR SICHUAN PEPPERCORNS IN ASIAN MARKETS OR ONLINE.

PLACE THE COOKED WONTONS IN A SERVING BOWL, AND DRIZZLE WITH RAYU.

WE DRIZZLE BOILED WONTONS WITH RAYU (P. 190) — THOUGH ANY CHILE OIL WILL WORK FINE — AND TOP WITH GROUND SICHUAN PEPPERCORNS, GREEN ONIONS, AND SESAME SEEDS FOR A FANTASTICALLY FLAVORFUL SENSATION!

SPRINKLE WITH GROUND SICHUAN PEPPERCORNS AS DESIRED, GREEN ONIONS, AND SESAME SEEDS AND SERVE.

a word about WONTON SOUP

IF YOU WERE ABLE TO SAVE SHRIMP HEADS AND SHELLS FROM MAKING WONTONS (P. 101), ADDING THEM TO THE BROTH WILL ADD A BIT OF OCEANIC DEPTH TO YOUR SOUP, BUT IF NOT, NO WORRIES!

EITHER WAY, USE A LOW-SODIUM STOCK (PREFERABLY HOMEMADE, P. 87) AND SEASON TO YOUR LIKING, VIEWING IT AS A LOW-DECIBEL BASE UPON WHICH YOU CAN BLAST YOUR WONTON SYMPHONY.

ADD COLOR, TEXTURE, AND NUTRITION WITH BLANCHED BOK CHOY OR OTHER GREENS!

WONTON SOUP

SERVES 4

INGREDIENTS:

2 TABLESPOONS NEUTRAL OIL (IF USING SHRIMP)

SHRIMP HEADS AND SHELLS RESERVED FROM MAKING WONTONS (OPTIONAL)

4 CUPS CHICKEN STOCK (P. 87) OR STORE-BOUGHT LOW-SODIUM CHICKEN BROTH

1 TABLESPOON SOY SAUCE

2 TEASPOONS TOASTED SESAME OIL

SALT

4 BABY BOK CHOY, HALVED LENGTHWISE

20 WONTONS (P. 101)

GROUND WHITE PEPPER (OPTIONAL)

BRING A LARGE POT OF SALTED WATER TO A BOIL.

IF USING SHRIMP HEADS AND SHELLS:

HEAT THE NEUTRAL OIL IN A MEDIUM POT OVER MEDIUM-HIGH HEAT UNTIL SHIMMERING.

ADD THE HEADS AND SHELLS TO THE POT, AND COOK, STIRRING, FOR 3 MINUTES, UNTIL FRAGRANT AND PINK.

ADD THE STOCK AND LOWER THE HEAT TO MAINTAIN A SIMMER; COOK FOR 5 MINUTES.

STRAIN OUT THE SHRIMP HEADS AND SHELLS AND DISCARD,

AND RETURN THE POT TO HEAT.

BRING THE STOCK TO A SIMMER

AND ADD SOY SAUCE AND SESAME OIL.

TASTE AND ADD SALT AS DESIRED.

MEANWHILE, BLANCH THE BOK CHOY IN BOILING WATER FOR 30 TO 45 SECONDS, UNTIL VIBRANT GREEN AND TENDER (BUT NOT SOFT),

THEN USE A SPIDER TO REMOVE THE BOK CHOY FROM THE POT AND LET DRAIN FOR A FEW SECONDS.

TRANSFER TO FOUR SOUP BOWLS, ALLOWING TWO HALVES PER BOWL.

BOIL THE WONTONS IN THE BOK CHOY WATER FOR 90 SECONDS, UNTIL THE FILLING IS COOKED THROUGH.

REMOVE THE WONTONS WITH A SPIDER AND PLACE FIVE WONTONS IN EACH BOWL.

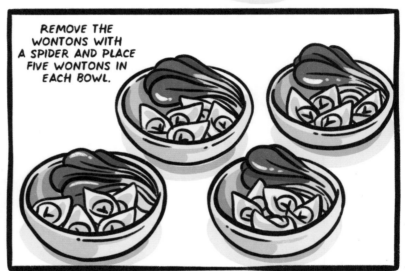

LADLE HOT SOUP EQUALLY AMONG THE BOWLS AND DUST CONSERVATIVELY WITH WHITE PEPPER, IF DESIRED.

SERVE IMMEDIATELY.

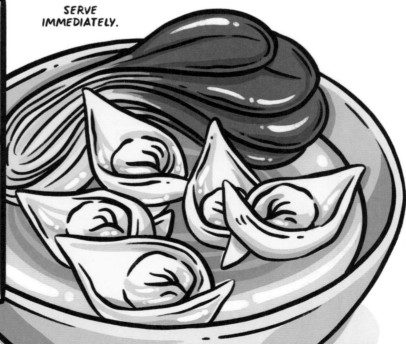

a word about SHUMAI

MANY VARIETIES OF SHUMAI EXIST ACROSS THE CUISINES OF CHINA (SOME USING MUTTON AND SOME USING GLUTINOUS RICE),

JAPAN (WITH A SMOOTH SHRIMP FILLING),

AND INDONESIA (SMOTHERED IN A PEANUT SAUCE),

BUT HERE WE FOCUS ON THE MOST COMMONLY FOUND CANTONESE DIM SUM FAVORITE,

FILLED WITH PORK, SHRIMP, MUSHROOMS, AND WATER CHESTNUTS.

SINCE THE WRAPPER DOESN'T NEED TO BE SEALED, YOU CAN STUFF MORE FILLING INTO SHUMAI THAN INTO THE AVERAGE SEALED DUMPLING.

GRATED CARROT OR A FRESH GREEN PEA WORKS GREAT AS A GARNISH,

BUT YOU CAN ALSO GET FANCY WITH THE FLYING FISH ROE KNOWN AS TOBIKO (AVAILABLE IN SPECIALTY STORES)!

PORK, SHRIMP & MUSHROOM SHUMAI

MAKES ABOUT 36 SHUMAI

INGREDIENTS:

1 TABLESPOON NEUTRAL OIL

8 OUNCES SHIITAKE MUSHROOMS, STEMMED AND MINCED

2 GARLIC CLOVES, MINCED

1 TEASPOON TOASTED SESAME OIL

12 OUNCES GROUND PORK

4 OUNCES SHRIMP, PEELED, DEVEINED, AND FINELY CHOPPED

½ CUP PEELED AND MINCED FRESH WATER CHESTNUTS (OR WELL-RINSED CANNED WATER CHESTNUTS)

2 GREEN ONIONS, TRIMMED AND MINCED

1½ TEASPOONS SALT

1 TEASPOON SUGAR

½ TEASPOON WHITE PEPPER

2 TABLESPOONS SOY SAUCE

1 EGG

36 STORE-BOUGHT GYOZA WRAPPERS OR HOMEMADE WONTON WRAPPERS (P. 31), CUT INTO 3-INCH ROUNDS

1 CARROT, PEELED AND GRATED ON THE FINE HOLES OF A BOX GRATER, OR FROZEN PEAS, OR TOBIKO ROE (OPTIONAL) TO GARNISH

HEAT THE NEUTRAL OIL IN A SMALL SAUTÉ PAN OVER MEDIUM-HIGH HEAT UNTIL SHIMMERING.

ADD THE MUSHROOMS AND GARLIC AND COOK, STIRRING OCCASIONALLY, FOR 3 TO 5 MINUTES, UNTIL FRAGRANT AND SOFTENING.

ADD THE SESAME OIL AND REMOVE FROM THE HEAT.

YOU CAN SUBSTITUTE 1½ OUNCES DRIED SHIITAKE, REHYDRATED IN HOT WATER FOR 30 MINUTES AND DRAINED WELL, FOR THE FRESH SHIITAKE.

SET ASIDE UNTIL COOLED TO ROOM TEMPERATURE.

PLACE THE COOLED MUSHROOM MIXTURE, PORK, SHRIMP, WATER CHESTNUTS, GREEN ONIONS, SALT, SUGAR, WHITE PEPPER, SOY SAUCE, AND EGG IN A MEDIUM BOWL.

WE PREFER FRESH WATER CHESTNUTS, FOUND IN ASIAN MARKETS, BUT YOU CAN SUBSTITUTE WELL-RINSED CANNED WATER CHESTNUTS AS WELL.

USE YOUR HAND TO VIGOROUSLY MIX THE FILLING UNTIL IT STARTS TO COME TOGETHER, 20 TO 30 SECONDS.

THEN "KNEAD" THE FILLING BY FOLDING IT OVER ON ITSELF REPEATEDLY FOR ANOTHER 90 SECONDS.

FINISH EMULSIFYING THE FILLING BY CONTINUOUSLY PICKING IT UP AND SLAPPING IT BACK DOWN INTO THE BOWL FOR ANOTHER 30 SECONDS.

THE MIXTURE SHOULD BE COHESIVE.

TO TRY THE FILLING, MICROWAVE ABOUT A TEASPOON OF IT FOR 20 TO 30 SECONDS AND ADJUST THE SEASONING TO TASTE.

FOLD!

FILL EACH WRAPPER WITH ABOUT 1 TABLESPOON OF FILLING, FOLD AS DIRECTED UNDER SHUMAI (P. 44),

AND TOP WITH A SMALL BIT OF GRATED CARROT OR A SINGLE GREEN PEA

(IF USING TOBIKO ROE, GARNISH AFTER COOKING).

COOK!

COOK AS SUGGESTED UNDER STEAMING (P. 52),

SHUMAI LOOSELY TRANSLATES TO "COOK/SELL," IMPLYING THAT THESE GUYS ARE BEST SOLD AND SERVED HOT OUT OF A STEAMER!

SERVE!

AND SERVE WITH A DESIRED SAUCE (WE LIKE BLACK VINEGAR DIPPING SAUCE, P. 182, OR SESAME-SOY DIPPING SAUCE, P. 185).

ALTERNATIVELY, FREEZE UNCOOKED (P. 62).

a word about CRAB RANGOON

THIS IS A FUN LITTLE APPETIZER KNOWN TO ANYONE WHO HAS ORDERED CHINESE TAKEOUT.

EVEN THOUGH ITS NAME IMPLIES BURMESE LINEAGE, ITS ACTUAL ORIGIN WAS MOST LIKELY FROM AN AMERICAN "POLYNESIAN" RESTAURANT IN THE 1950s: TRADER VIC'S.

MAYBE THERE WAS A BURMESE RECIPE THAT INSPIRED CRAB RANGOON, BUT GIVEN THAT CHEESES ARE RARE IN CHINA AND BURMA, THIS DUMPLING SCREAMS AMERICAN INVENTION.

EITHER WAY, WE CAN SIMPLY ENJOY IT FOR THE CRISPY DEEP-FRIED BUNDLE OF CREAM CHEESE THAT IT IS!

WE PREFER TO USE SURIMI, OR IMITATION CRABMEAT, HERE — REAL CRAB IS NOT ONLY EXPENSIVE, BUT IT CAN OVERPOWER THE CREAM CHEESE.

FOLD USING THE 4-POINTED STAR TECHNIQUE (P. 39) FOR MORE CRUNCHY, CRISPY DIPPING POWER!

CRAB RANGOON

MAKES ABOUT 48 CRAB RANGOON

INGREDIENTS:

8 OUNCES CREAM CHEESE, PREFERABLY AT ROOM TEMPERATURE

8 OUNCES SURIMI (IMITATION CRABMEAT), COARSELY CHOPPED, OR SHREDDED BACKFIN OR LUMP CRABMEAT

2 GREEN ONIONS, TRIMMED AND MINCED

½ TEASPOON LEMON JUICE (OPTIONAL)

½ TEASPOON SALT

48 SQUARE STORE-BOUGHT WONTON WRAPPERS OR HOMEMADE WONTON WRAPPERS (P. 40)

NEUTRAL OIL FOR DEEP-FRYING

PLACE THE CREAM CHEESE, SURIMI, GREEN ONIONS, LEMON JUICE (IF USING), AND SALT IN A MEDIUM BOWL.

MIX WELL WITH A LARGE SPOON OR YOUR HAND UNTIL FULLY COMBINED.

TASTE AND ADJUST THE SEASONING AS DESIRED.

NORMALLY CREAM CHEESE DOESN'T FREEZE THAT WELL, BUT IT WORKS JUST FINE FOR THIS RECIPE!

SO IF NOT COOKING IMMEDIATELY, FILL AND FOLD YOUR CRAB RANGOON AND FREEZE UNCOOKED (P. 62).

UNUSED FILLING CAN BE KEPT REFRIGERATED FOR UP TO 5 DAYS.

FOLD!

FILL EACH WRAPPER WITH ABOUT 2 TEASPOONS OF FILLING AND FOLD AS DIRECTED FOR 4-POINTED STARS (P. 39).

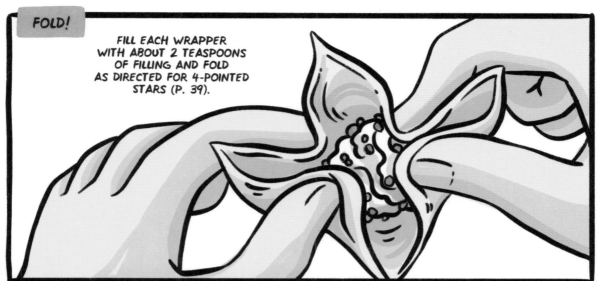

COOK!

DEEP-FRY IN BATCHES UNTIL GOLDEN BROWN AS DIRECTED UNDER DEEP-FRYING (P. 59)

IF FRYING FROM A FROZEN STATE, BEWARE OF DANGEROUS SPLATTERS!

SERVE!

AND SERVE IMMEDIATELY WITH DUCK SAUCE (P. 188) OR SWEET CHILE SAUCE (P. 186).

a word about MOMOS

THESE TRADITIONAL TIBETAN DUMPLINGS CAN BE FOUND WITH ALL KINDS OF FILLINGS, INCLUDING GOAT, LAMB, YAK, OR EVEN PANEER CHEESE,

AND THEY CAN BE FOLDED INTO PLEATED CRESCENTS OR — PREFERABLY — LOVELY LITTLE PURSES.

SOMETIMES MOMOS ARE SERVED IN A RICH SOUP,

BUT WE THINK THE FLAVORS REALLY COME THROUGH WHEN THEY'RE STEAMED AND SERVED ALONGSIDE THE TIBETAN CHILE HOT SAUCE KNOWN AS SEPEN (P. 192).

WE'RE ALSO SUSCEPTIBLE TO THE INDULGENT DELIGHT OF A PAN-FRIED OR DEEP-FRIED MOMO!

TIBETAN BEEF MOMOS

MAKES ABOUT 48 MOMOS

INGREDIENTS:

1 POUND GROUND BEEF

1 SMALL ONION, GRATED ON THE SMALL HOLES OF A BOX GRATER, JUICES INCLUDED

½ CUP MINCED CILANTRO, STEMS INCLUDED, OR MORE OR LESS TO TASTE

3 GARLIC CLOVES, PEELED AND MINCED ON A MICROPLANE

2-INCH PIECE GINGER, PEELED AND MINCED ON A MICROPLANE

1 TEASPOON SUGAR

1 TEASPOON SALT

1 TEASPOON FRESHLY GROUND BLACK PEPPER

1½ TEASPOONS SOY SAUCE

1 TEASPOON RICE VINEGAR

48 HOMEMADE DUMPLING WRAPPERS (P. 27) OR STORE-BOUGHT GYOZA WRAPPERS

NEUTRAL OIL FOR PAN-FRYING OR DEEP-FRYING (OPTIONAL)

TO MAKE THE FILLING, COMBINE THE BEEF, ONION, CILANTRO, GARLIC, GINGER, SUGAR, SALT, PEPPER, SOY SAUCE, AND VINEGAR IN A LARGE BOWL.

USE YOUR HAND TO VIGOROUSLY MIX THE FILLING UNTIL IT STARTS TO COME TOGETHER, 20 TO 30 SECONDS.

GRATING AN ONION WILL RUPTURE ITS CELLS AND EXPOSE MORE ONIONY GOODNESS FOR AN INTENSE ONION FLAVOR (AND SMOOTHER TEXTURE) IN THE FINISHED MOMOS!

THEN "KNEAD" THE FILLING BY FOLDING IT OVER ON ITSELF REPEATEDLY FOR ANOTHER 90 SECONDS.

TO TRY THE FILLING, MICROWAVE ABOUT A TEASPOON OF IT FOR 20 TO 30 SECONDS AND ADJUST THE SEASONING TO TASTE.

THE MIXTURE SHOULD BE COHESIVE AND WON'T NEED THE FORCEFUL SLAPPING MOTION USED IN THE WETTER PORK-BASED FILLINGS.

THE FILLING CAN BE FROZEN AT THIS POINT IN AN AIRTIGHT CONTAINER FOR UP TO 2 MONTHS.

FOLD!

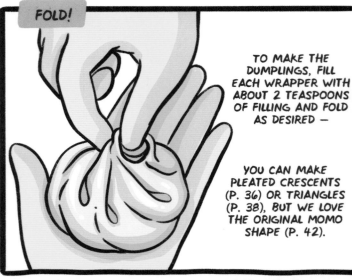

TO MAKE THE DUMPLINGS, FILL EACH WRAPPER WITH ABOUT 2 TEASPOONS OF FILLING AND FOLD AS DESIRED —

YOU CAN MAKE PLEATED CRESCENTS (P. 36) OR TRIANGLES (P. 38), BUT WE LOVE THE ORIGINAL MOMO SHAPE (P. 42).

COOK!

COOK AS DESIRED: WE LIKE STEAMING (P. 52), DEEP-FRYING (P. 59), OR PAN-FRYING (P. 56).

SERVE!

SERVE ALONGSIDE TIBETAN SEPEN SPICY CHILE SAUCE (P. 192).

ALTERNATIVELY, FREEZE UNCOOKED MOMOS (P. 62).

a word about BUUZ

MONGOLIA'S HARSH CLIMATE RESULTS IN DELICIOUSLY ROBUST FOOD TO MATCH.

MONGOLIAN DUMPLINGS ARE A PRODUCT OF THE REGION'S AGRICULTURAL DEPENDENCE ON HARDY LIVESTOCK AND VEGETABLES.

BUUZ ARE FILLED WITH RICHLY FLAVORED LAMB ACCOMPANIED WITH SIMPLE INGREDIENTS (WE MAKE OURS WITH ONION, CARROT, AND GARLIC).

YOU CAN SUBSTITUTE BEEF IF YOU REALLY WANT TO, BUT WHICHEVER MEAT YOU DECIDE TO USE, WE RECOMMEND STICKING WITH A FATTIER BLEND FOR MAXIMUM RICHNESS DURING THE COLD WINTER MONTHS!

MONGOLIAN LAMB BUUZ

MAKES ABOUT 48 BUUZ

INGREDIENTS:

1 POUND GROUND LAMB OR MUTTON

1 MEDIUM ONION, GRATED ON THE SMALL HOLES OF A BOX GRATER, JUICES INCLUDED

1 LARGE CARROT, PEELED AND GRATED ON THE SMALL HOLES OF A BOX GRATER

3 GARLIC CLOVES, PEELED AND GRATED ON A MICROPLANE

2 TEASPOONS SALT

1 TEASPOON FRESHLY GROUND BLACK PEPPER

1 TEASPOON RICE VINEGAR

48 HOMEMADE DUMPLING WRAPPERS (P. 27) OR STORE-BOUGHT GYOZA WRAPPERS

MUTTON IS SIMPLY A TERM FOR THE MEAT OF AN ADULT SHEEP — IT IS HARD TO FIND BUT FULL OF ASSERTIVE LAMB FLAVOR!

PLACE THE LAMB, ONION, CARROT, GARLIC, SALT, PEPPER, AND VINEGAR IN A LARGE BOWL.

USE YOUR HAND TO VIGOROUSLY MIX THE FILLING UNTIL IT STARTS TO COME TOGETHER, 20 TO 30 SECONDS.

THEN "KNEAD" THE FILLING BY FOLDING IT OVER ON ITSELF REPEATEDLY FOR ANOTHER 90 SECONDS.

THE MIXTURE SHOULD BE COHESIVE AND WON'T NEED THE FORCEFUL SLAPPING MOTION USED IN THE WETTER PORK-BASED FILLINGS.

TO TRY THE FILLING, MICROWAVE ABOUT A TEASPOON OF IT FOR 20 TO 30 SECONDS AND ADJUST THE SEASONING TO TASTE.

THE FILLING CAN BE FROZEN AT THIS POINT IN AN AIRTIGHT CONTAINER FOR UP TO 2 MONTHS.

FOLD!

FILL THE WRAPPERS WITH ABOUT 2 TEASPOONS OF FILLING EACH AND FOLD AS DESIRED — THE MOMO SHAPE (P. 42) WORKS GREAT, AS DOES THE PLEATED CRESCENT (P. 36).

COOK!

BUUZ SHOULD BE STEAMED (P. 52), ALL THE BETTER IF YOU DO SO OVER A BIG CAULDRON OF BUBBLING LAMB SOUP!

ALTERNATIVELY, FREEZE BUUZ UNCOOKED (P. 62).

SERVE!

TYPICALLY, THESE WOULDN'T BE SERVED WITH A SAUCE, BUT WHY NOT BE ATYPICAL AND SERVE THEM WITH A SAUCE FROM SOMEWHERE NEARBY: TIBETAN SEPAN (P. 192)?

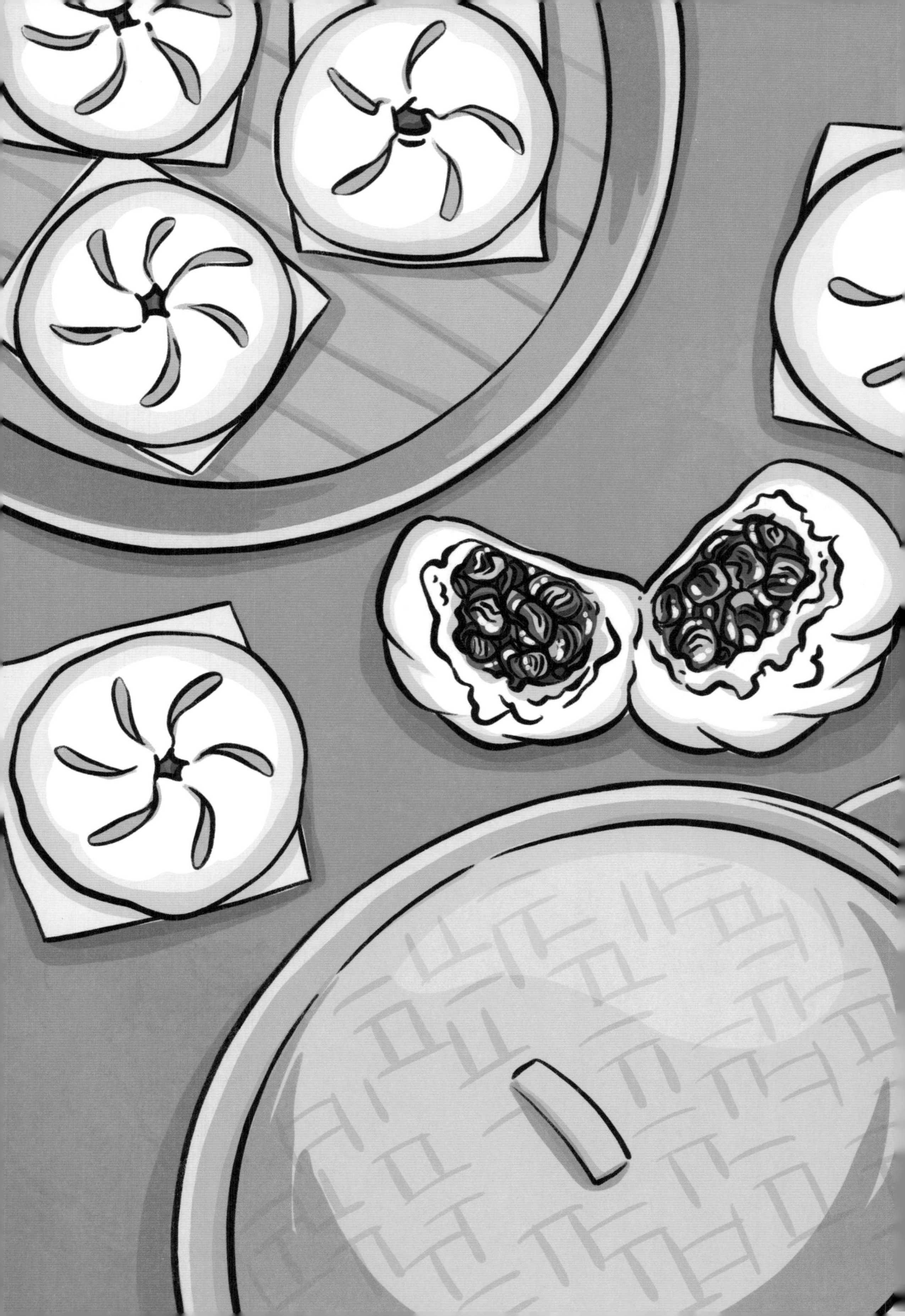

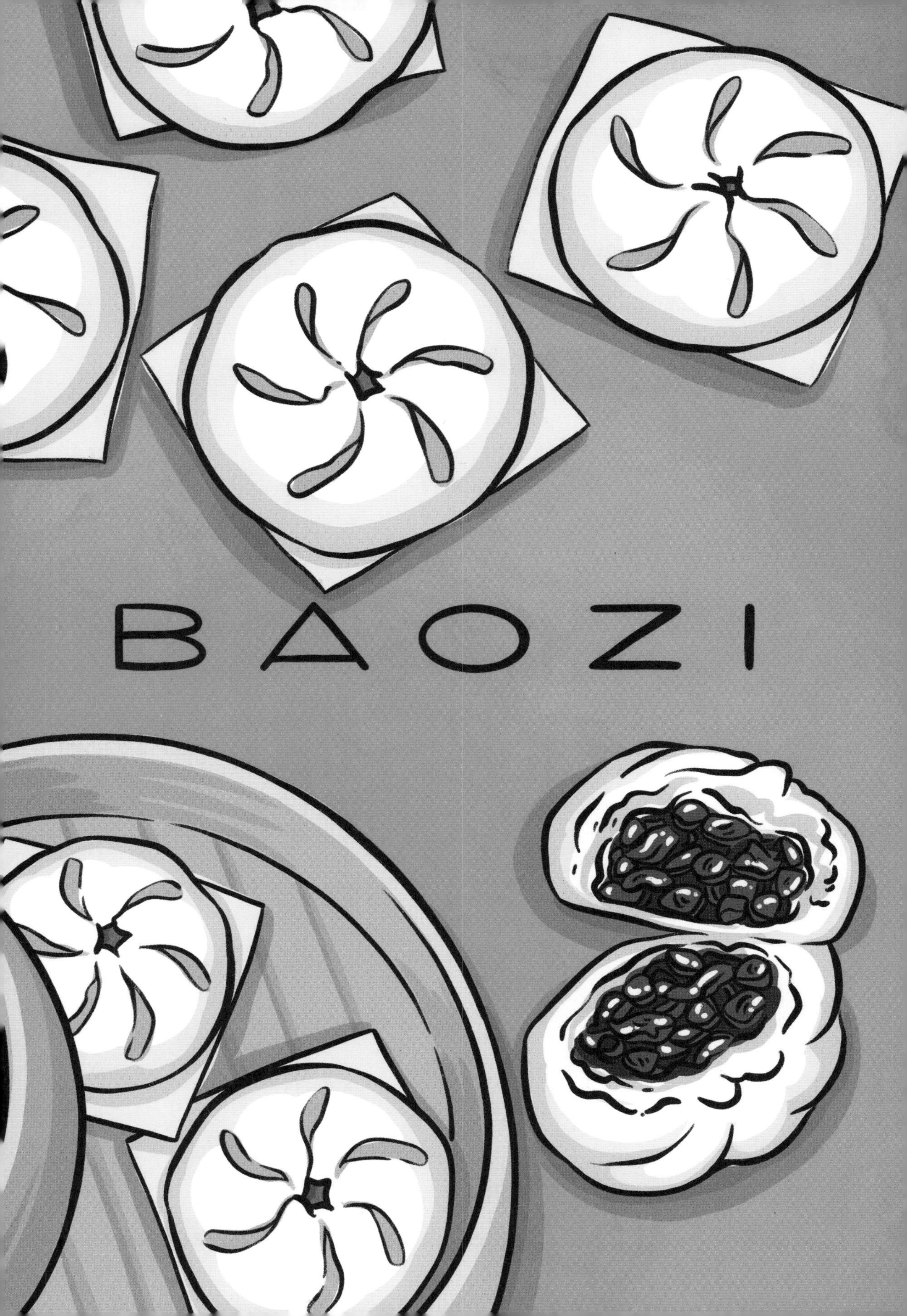
BAOZI

a word about BAOZI

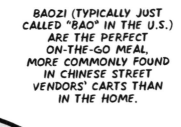

BAOZI (TYPICALLY JUST CALLED "BAO" IN THE U.S.) ARE THE PERFECT ON-THE-GO MEAL, MORE COMMONLY FOUND IN CHINESE STREET VENDORS' CARTS THAN IN THE HOME.

DEVELOPED IN A PART OF THE WORLD WHERE STEAMING APPARATUS ARE MORE PREVALENT THAN OVENS,

BAOZI ARE SATISFYINGLY SOFT AND CHEWY STEAMED YEAST BREADS.

STUFFED WITH DYNAMICALLY FLAVORED FILLINGS, BAOZI ARE LARGER AND MORE SUBSTANTIAL THAN MOST OTHER DUMPLINGS.

OFTEN THOUGH, THE STEAMED DOUGH IS LEFT FLAT AND UNFILLED

AND SERVED ALONGSIDE SLICED PORK OR OTHER TASTY TOPPINGS SO DINERS CAN BUILD THEIR BUNS ACCORDING TO THEIR TASTES.

OUR BAOZI DOUGH CAN CERTAINLY BE ROLLED FLAT AND STEAMED IN THIS STYLE, BUT IN THIS BOOK, WE'LL STICK TO THE FILLED AND SEALED DUMPLINGS!

BAOZI

INGREDIENTS:

1 (¼ OUNCE) PACKET OR 2¼ TEASPOONS INSTANT OR QUICK-RISING YEAST

1 CUP WATER, JUST WARM TO THE TOUCH

450 GRAMS (ABOUT 3 CUPS) ALL-PURPOSE FLOUR

2 TABLESPOONS SUGAR

1 TABLESPOON BAKING POWDER

1 TEASPOON SALT

3 TABLESPOONS NEUTRAL OIL OR ROOM-TEMPERATURE LARD

2 CUPS OF YOUR CHOICE OF CHAR SIU (P. 128), CURRIED BEEF (P. 132), KUNG PAO CHICKEN (P. 135), OR SAVORY MUSHROOMS (P. 139)

BAOZI DOUGH IS SUPER SIMPLE AND CAN BE THROWN TOGETHER IN MINUTES — JUST BE SURE TO GIVE IT THE TIME IT NEEDS TO RISE BOTH BEFORE AND AFTER FILLING!

WITH CHOPSTICKS, STIR THE YEAST INTO THE WATER.

SET ASIDE.

COMBINE THE FLOUR, SUGAR, BAKING POWDER, AND SALT IN A LARGE BOWL.

WHILE STIRRING THE FLOUR MIXTURE WITH CHOPSTICKS, SLOWLY ADD THE YEAST MIXTURE,

THEN THE OIL OR FAT (IF USING LARD, THE MIXTURE WILL REMAIN A BIT CLUMPY UNTIL KNEADED).

WHEN WELL COMBINED, USE YOUR HANDS TO SCRAPE EXCESS DOUGH FROM THE CHOPSTICKS.

KNEAD THE DOUGH AGAINST THE SIDE OF THE BOWL.

WHEN THE DOUGH IS ONE COHESIVE PIECE, AND ALL CRUMBS AND FLOUR HAVE BEEN INCORPORATED, CONTINUE KNEADING UNTIL THE DOUGH IS SMOOTH, ABOUT 3 MINUTES.

TUCK IN THE EDGES OF THE DOUGH TO FORM A BALL WITH A SMOOTH, TIGHT SURFACE.

LIGHTLY OIL A BOWL

AND PLACE THE DOUGH IN IT, SMOOTH ROUNDED-SIDE UP.

COVER THE BOWL WITH PLASTIC WRAP AND LEAVE THE DOUGH TO RISE IN A WARM SPOT UNTIL DOUBLED IN SIZE, 45 MINUTES TO 1 HOUR.

THE DOUGH IS NOW READY TO FILL AND SHAPE.

IF YOU PREFER, YOU CAN PUNCH DOWN THE DOUGH UNTIL IT IS ABOUT 1 INCH THICK AND REFRIGERATE IT FOR UP TO 1 DAY, LETTING IT SIT AT ROOM TEMPERATURE FOR 1 HOUR BEFORE PROCEEDING AGAIN WHEN READY.

TO FILL AND SHAPE BAOZI, PLACE HALF OF THE RISEN DOUGH BALL ON A LIGHTLY FLOURED SURFACE

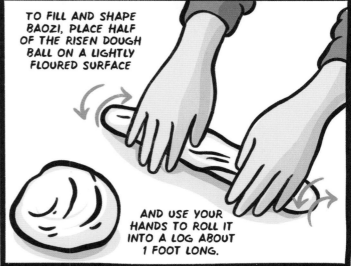

AND USE YOUR HANDS TO ROLL IT INTO A LOG ABOUT 1 FOOT LONG.

CUT THE LOG IN HALF,

THEN CUT EACH HALF IN HALF SO YOU HAVE FOUR PIECES.

CUT EACH OF THESE FOUR PIECES IN HALF AGAIN

THEN REPEAT THE PROCESS WITH THE RESERVED HALF OF DOUGH SO YOU HAVE 16 EQUAL PIECES IN TOTAL.

SET EACH DOUGH PIECE ON ITS CUT SIDE,

GIVE IT A LITTLE PINCH TO SHAPE IT INTO A DISC,

AND FLATTEN IT AS MUCH AS POSSIBLE WITH THE HEEL OF YOUR HAND.

USING A SMALL WOODEN DOWEL (SEE EQUIPMENT, P. 20) OR A ROLLING PIN ON A LIGHTLY FLOURED SURFACE, ROLL EACH PIECE OF DOUGH INTO A ROUND ABOUT 4 INCHES IN DIAMETER.

PLACE ABOUT 2 TABLESPOONS OF YOUR CHOICE OF FILLING IN THE MIDDLE OF EACH PIECE OF DOUGH, LEAVING ABOUT ½ INCH OF DOUGH AROUND THE FILLING.

BEGIN SHAPING BY USING THE MOMO FOLDING STYLE (P. 42),

BUT FINISH BY GIVING THE TOP A SQUEEZE AND TWIST TO SEAL THE BAOZI COMPLETELY.

NOTE THAT BAOZI DOUGH RISES BEST WHEN FRESH, SO PROOF AND COOK IMMEDIATELY!

PLACE EACH BAOZI ON AN INDIVIDUAL SQUARE OF PARCHMENT PAPER AND SET THEM IN STEAMER BASKETS,

LEAVING 1 INCH AROUND EACH ONE FOR SPACE TO RISE AS THEY PROOF AND COOK.

COVER THE STEAMER BASKET WITH PLASTIC WRAP

AND LET THE BAOZI RISE IN A WARM SPOT UNTIL DOUBLED IN SIZE, ABOUT 30 MINUTES.

REMOVE THE PLASTIC AND STEAM AS DIRECTED UNDER STEAMING (P. 52) FOR 10 TO 15 MINUTES, UNTIL THE DOUGH IS COOKED THROUGH AND THE FILLING IS HOT.

SERVE IMMEDIATELY — THE FILLINGS ARE QUITE FLAVORFUL, BUT SWEET CHILE SAUCE (P. 186) ALWAYS GOES WELL WITH BAOZI!

CHAR SIU FOR BAOZI

INGREDIENTS:

1 BUNCH GREEN ONIONS, TRIMMED AND HALVED CROSSWISE

6 GARLIC CLOVES, SMASHED AND PEELED

1 ARBOL CHILE

¼ PACKED CUP DARK BROWN SUGAR

½ TEASPOON CHINESE FIVE-SPICE POWDER

1 CUP MIRIN (SEE PANTRY, P. 19)

1 CUP SAKE OR DRY WHITE WINE

¼ CUP RICE VINEGAR

¾ CUP SOY SAUCE

2 POUNDS BONELESS PORK SHOULDER, CUT INTO 1-INCH CUBES

DOUGH FROM BAOZI (P. 123)

COMBINE THE GREEN ONIONS, GARLIC, CHILE, BROWN SUGAR, FIVE-SPICE POWDER, MIRIN, SAKE, RICE VINEGAR, AND SOY SAUCE IN A MEDIUM SAUCEPAN

TRADITIONAL CHINESE CHAR SIU GETS MARINATED IN A SWEET, DISTINCTIVELY RED SAUCE BEFORE BEING ROASTED OR GRILLED OVER AN OPEN FIRE.

AND BRING TO A BOIL OVER MEDIUM-HIGH HEAT.

ENTHUSIASTS OF JAPANESE RAMEN WILL BE MORE FAMILIAR WITH CHASHU, A SIMILARLY SUCCULENT PIECE OF PORK BRAISED IN SOY SAUCE, VINEGAR, AND SAKE.

SINCE WE'LL BE CHOPPING THE CHAR SIU FOR BAOZI, WE CAN CUT THE PORK INTO SMALL CUBES BEFORE MARINATING TO INCREASE THE SURFACE AREA FOR A MORE GLAZY, CRISPY COATING!

LOWER THE HEAT TO MAINTAIN A RAPID SIMMER AND REDUCE THE LIQUID TO ABOUT ONE-QUARTER ITS ORIGINAL VOLUME, 15 TO 25 MINUTES.

OUR VERSION OF CHAR SIU HERE CONCENTRATES FLAVORS FROM BOTH STYLES FOR A STRONG MARINADE THAT GLAZES THE PORK AS IT ROASTS, SIMPLIFYING THE PROCESS INTO TWO EASY STEPS FOR A GREAT BAOZI FILLING.

REMOVE FROM THE HEAT AND LET COOL FULLY.

STRAIN AND DISCARD THE SOLIDS.

PUT THE PORK IN A RESEALABLE BAG AND ADD THE COOLED MARINADE.

SQUEEZE AS MUCH AIR FROM THE BAG AS POSSIBLE AND SEAL,

MASSAGING THE SO THE MARINADE IS DISTRIBUTED EVENLY.

REFRIGERATE FOR AT LEAST 24 HOURS, OR UP TO 48 HOURS.

PREHEAT THE OVEN TO 450°F.

LINE A BAKING SHEET WITH ALUMINUM FOIL AND TOP WITH A COOLING RACK.

THE FOIL WILL KEEP YOUR PAN CLEAN — JUST BE AWARE THAT THE MARINADE AND JUICES THAT DRIP ONTO THE PAN COULD CREATE SOME SMOKE — TURN ON YOUR FANS AND OPEN YOUR WINDOWS!

REMOVE THE PORK FROM THE MARINADE AND PLACE ON THE RACK.

STRAIN THE REMAINING MARINADE THROUGH A FINE-MESH STRAINER INTO A SMALL SAUCEPAN.

BRING TO A SIMMER OVER HIGH HEAT

AND COOK FOR 3 MINUTES TO MAKE THE MARINADE SAFE TO USE AS A SAUCE;

SET ASIDE WITH A BRUSH FOR GLAZING THE PORK.

PLACE THE TRAY IN THE OVEN AND ROAST THE PORK.

ALTERNATIVELY, YOU CAN COOK THE PORK ON A HIGH-HEAT GRILL, TURNING IT FROM TIME TO TIME TO AVOID BURNING.

TURN THE PORK AND BRUSH WITH THE MARINADE EVERY 5 MINUTES

UNTIL NICELY GLAZED ON THE OUTSIDE AND COOKED THROUGH ON THE INSIDE TO A ROSY HUE (ABOUT 140°F).

REMOVE FROM THE OVEN AND LET COOL

BEFORE CHOPPING COARSELY

AND USING AS A FILLING AS DIRECTED IN BAOZI (P. 123).

ALTERNATIVELY, STORE THE FILLING IN THE REFRIGERATOR FOR UP TO 5 DAYS OR FREEZE FOR UP TO 3 MONTHS.

CURRIED BEEF FOR BAOZI

INGREDIENTS:

2 TABLESPOONS CURRY POWDER

2 TABLESPOONS SALT

2 POUNDS BONELESS BEEF CHUCK, CUT INTO 2-INCH CUBES

2 TABLESPOONS NEUTRAL OIL OR LARD

1 LARGE ONION, CUT INTO LARGE DICE

6 GARLIC CLOVES, SMASHED WITH THE SIDE OF A KNIFE

3-INCH PIECE GINGER, UNPEELED AND SLICED 1/4 INCH THICK

1 ARBOL CHILE (OPTIONAL)

1 STAR ANISE

1 TABLESPOON WHOLE BLACK PEPPERCORNS

1 CUP SAKE OR DRY WHITE WINE

1 CUP WATER

1/2 CUP SOY SAUCE

2 TABLESPOONS TOASTED SESAME OIL

1 TABLESPOON RICE VINEGAR

DOUGH FROM BAOZI (P. 123)

MIX THE CURRY POWDER AND SALT IN A MEDIUM BOWL,

THEN ADD THE BEEF AND RUB ALL OVER.

THIS FILLING IS GREAT ATOP PLAIN STEAMED RICE AS WELL AS INSIDE A SOFT BAOZI BUN.

A DELICIOUS STOCK IS MADE IN THE COOKING PROCESS, SO BE SURE TO SAVE THAT FOR ANOTHER USE!

COVER AND LET SIT, REFRIGERATED, FOR AT LEAST 1 HOUR, OR UP TO OVERNIGHT.

HEAT A HEAVY DUTCH OVEN OVER MEDIUM-HIGH HEAT AND ADD THE OIL.

DISCARD ANY EXCESS RUB

AND SEAR THE BEEF ON A FEW SIDES, ABOUT 1 MINUTE PER SIDE (BE CAREFUL NOT TO LET THE CURRY POWDER BURN) FOR A TOTAL OF ABOUT 3 MINUTES.

ADD THE ONION, GARLIC, AND GINGER AND COOK FOR ANOTHER 3 MINUTES, STIRRING FREQUENTLY.

ADD THE CHILE (IF USING), STAR ANISE, PEPPERCORNS, SAKE, WATER, SOY SAUCE, SESAME OIL, AND VINEGAR,

LOWER THE HEAT TO MAINTAIN A SIMMER, COVER,

AND COOK UNTIL THE MEAT IS TENDER AND A CHOPSTICK CAN EASILY BE INSERTED INTO IT (WITH AN INTERNAL TEMPERATURE OF ABOUT 190°F), 1 TO 1½ HOURS.

REMOVE FROM THE HEAT AND LET SIT UNTIL COOL ENOUGH TO HANDLE.

REMOVE THE BEEF AND STRAIN THE BROTH, DISCARDING ALL OTHER SOLIDS.

CHOP THE BEEF INTO FINE PIECES

AND MIX WITH A FEW TABLESPOONS OF ITS COOKING LIQUID.

LET COOL FULLY BEFORE USING AS A FILLING AS DIRECTED IN BAOZI (P. 123).

THE COOKING LIQUID MAY BE REFRIGERATED FOR UP TO 5 DAYS OR FROZEN FOR UP TO 3 MONTHS.

ALTERNATIVELY, STORE THE FILLING IN THE REFRIGERATOR FOR UP TO 5 DAYS OR FREEZE FOR UP TO 3 MONTHS.

KUNG PAO CHICKEN FOR BAOZI

MAKES 16 BAOZI, WITH LEFTOVERS

INGREDIENTS:

8 GARLIC CLOVES
(2 CLOVES MINCED AND
6 CLOVES THINLY SLICED)

3-INCH PIECE PEELED
GINGER (1 INCH MINCED
AND 2 INCHES FINELY
JULIENNED)

4 TABLESPOONS
SOY SAUCE

2 TABLESPOONS
SHAOXING WINE
(SEE PANTRY, P. 19)

1 TABLESPOON PLUS
2 TEASPOONS CORNSTARCH

2 POUNDS BONELESS,
SKINLESS CHICKEN
THIGHS, CUT INTO
½-INCH CUBES

2 TABLESPOONS BLACK
CHINKIANG VINEGAR
(SEE PANTRY, P. 18)

2 TEASPOONS SUGAR

¼ CUP NEUTRAL OIL

12 TO 15 ARBOL CHILES

1 TEASPOON SICHUAN
PEPPERCORNS, GROUND
AND SIFTED AS IN MA LA
WONTONS (P. 103)

4 GREEN ONIONS,
TRIMMED, SMASHED
WITH THE SIDE OF A
KNIFE, AND CUT INTO
1-INCH SEGMENTS

2 STALKS CELERY,
FINELY DICED

½ CUP ROASTED,
SALTED PEANUTS

DOUGH FROM BAOZI
(P. 123)

COMBINE THE MINCED GARLIC, MINCED GINGER, 2 TABLESPOONS OF THE SOY SAUCE, THE WINE, AND 1 TABLESPOON OF THE CORNSTARCH IN A MEDIUM BOWL AND MIX WELL.

ADD THE CHICKEN AND TOSS THOROUGHLY TO COAT.

THIS CLASSIC CHICKEN RECIPE IS GREAT EATEN ON ITS OWN OR WITH STEAMED RICE, BUT IS ABSOLUTELY DELICIOUS STUFFED INSIDE A BAOZI.

WHEN CUTTING INGREDIENTS, REMEMBER THE PIECES NEED TO BE SMALL ENOUGH TO FIT INSIDE THE BAOZI!

SET ASIDE.

COMBINE THE REMAINING 2 TABLESPOONS SOY SAUCE, THE BLACK VINEGAR, SUGAR, AND REMAINING 2 TEASPOONS CORNSTARCH IN A SMALL BOWL AND WHISK TO THOROUGHLY COMBINE.

SET ASIDE.

PLACE A WOK OR LARGE SKILLET OVER HIGH HEAT.

WHEN SMOKING, ADD THE OIL THEN THE CHILES AND PEPPERCORNS,

BREAK THE ARBOL CHILES IN HALF FOR MORE HEAT — JUST REMEMBER TO PICK THEM OUT BEFORE FILLING THE BAOZI TO AVOID ANY UNEXPECTED BLASTS OF HEAT!

STIR QUICKLY,

AND IMMEDIATELY ADD THE CHICKEN.

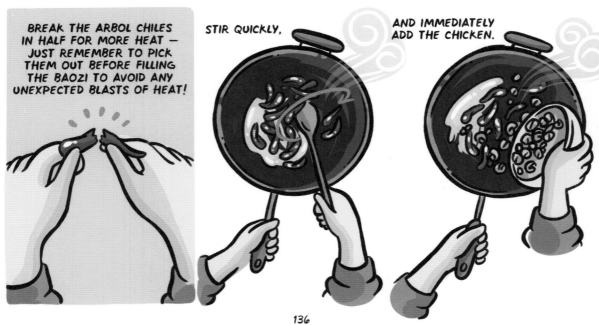

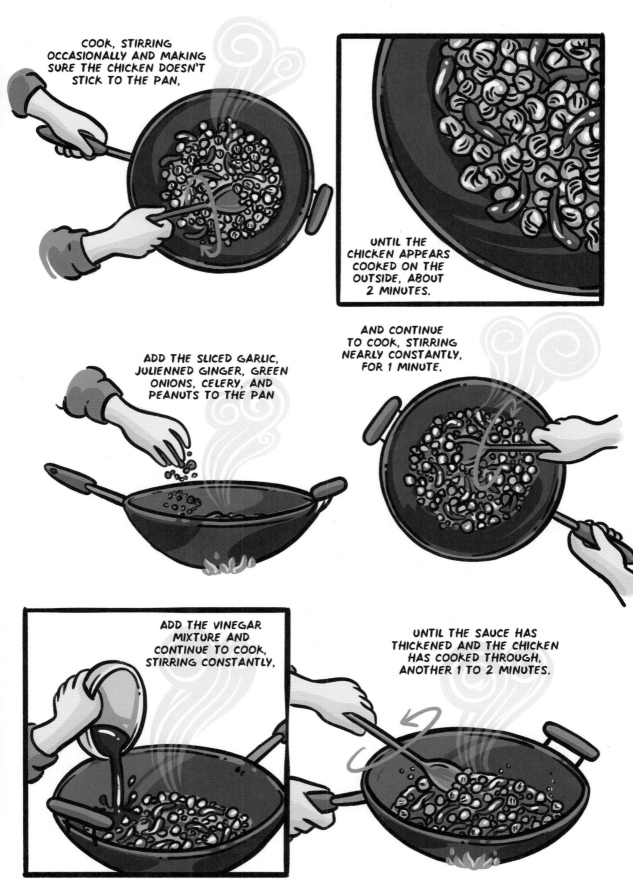

COOK, STIRRING OCCASIONALLY AND MAKING SURE THE CHICKEN DOESN'T STICK TO THE PAN,

UNTIL THE CHICKEN APPEARS COOKED ON THE OUTSIDE, ABOUT 2 MINUTES.

ADD THE SLICED GARLIC, JULIENNED GINGER, GREEN ONIONS, CELERY, AND PEANUTS TO THE PAN

AND CONTINUE TO COOK, STIRRING NEARLY CONSTANTLY, FOR 1 MINUTE.

ADD THE VINEGAR MIXTURE AND CONTINUE TO COOK, STIRRING CONSTANTLY,

UNTIL THE SAUCE HAS THICKENED AND THE CHICKEN HAS COOKED THROUGH, ANOTHER 1 TO 2 MINUTES.

REMOVE FROM HEAT AND LET COOL FULLY,

THEN REMOVE THE ARBOL CHILES AND DISCARD.

USE AS A FILLING AS DIRECTED IN BAOZI (P. 123).

ALTERNATIVELY, STORE IN AN AIRTIGHT CONTAINER IN THE REFRIGERATOR FOR UP TO 5 DAYS OR FREEZE FOR UP TO 1 MONTH.

SAVORY MUSHROOMS FOR BAOZI

MAKES 16 BAOZI, WITH LEFTOVERS

INGREDIENTS:

1 OUNCE DRIED SHIITAKE MUSHROOMS

1 TEASPOON SUGAR

1 TABLESPOON CORNSTARCH

3 TABLESPOONS SHAOXING WINE (SEE PANTRY, P. 19)

2 TABLESPOONS SOY SAUCE

1 TEASPOON RICE VINEGAR

2 TABLESPOONS NEUTRAL OIL

3 POUNDS MUSHROOMS (A MIX OF CRIMINI AND BUTTON), THINLY SLICED

½ TEASPOON SALT

4 GARLIC CLOVES, MINCED

2-INCH PIECE GINGER, PEELED AND MINCED

4 GREEN ONIONS, TRIMMED, WHITES MINCED AND GREENS THINLY SLICED ON THE DIAGONAL

DOUGH FROM BAOZI (P. 123)

PUT THE DRIED SHIITAKE IN A SMALL BOWL AND COVER WITH BOILING WATER.

LET SOAK FOR 15 MINUTES TO REHYDRATE.

THIS VEGETARIAN FILLING IS RICH AND SATISFYING — PERFECT FOR A MEAT-FREE BAOZI.

THE CRIMINI AND BUTTON MUSHROOMS PROVIDE SNAP AND BODY TO THE FILLING, AND THE DRIED SHIITAKE BRING HOME THAT STRONG UMAMI MUSHROOM FLAVOR.

THEN STRAIN, RESERVING THE LIQUID.

FINELY CHOP THE REHYDRATED MUSHROOMS

AND SET ASIDE.

MIX THE SUGAR, CORNSTARCH, WINE, SOY SAUCE, AND VINEGAR IN A SMALL BOWL AND SET ASIDE.

HEAT A LARGE SKILLET OVER MEDIUM-HIGH HEAT.

ADD THE OIL, THEN THE MIXED CRIMINI AND BUTTON MUSHROOMS ALONG WITH THE SALT.

SAUTÉ UNTIL THE MUSHROOMS BEGIN TO SOFTEN AND THE LIQUID THEY RELEASE NEARLY EVAPORATES FROM THE PAN, 7 TO 8 MINUTES.

ADD THE GARLIC, GINGER, AND GREEN ONION WHITES AND COOK UNTIL VERY AROMATIC, ABOUT 1 MINUTE.

ADD THE REHYDRATED MUSHROOMS AND ½ CUP OF THE MUSHROOM SOAKING WATER

AND COOK UNTIL THE LIQUID HAS NEARLY EVAPORATED COMPLETELY, 1 TO 3 MINUTES MORE.

140

STIR THE
SOY SAUCE
MIXTURE WELL

AND ADD IT TO
THE PAN, STIRRING
UNTIL INCORPORATED
AND SAUCY,
1 TO 2 MINUTES.

REMOVE FROM
THE HEAT AND
STIR IN THE
REMAINING
GREEN ONIONS.

TASTE AND ADJUST
THE SEASONING
AS DESIRED.

LET COOL FULLY
BEFORE USING AS
DIRECTED IN BAOZI
(P. 123).

THIS RECIPE DOESN'T
FREEZE WELL, BUT
YOU CAN STORE IT IN
THE REFRIGERATOR
FOR UP TO 5 DAYS.

SHENG JIAN BAOZI

MAKES ABOUT 32 BAOZI

INGREDIENTS:

1 POUND GROUND PORK

3 GREEN ONIONS, TRIMMED AND MINCED

3-INCH PIECE GINGER, PEELED AND GRATED ON A MICROPLANE

3 GARLIC CLOVES, PEELED AND GRATED ON A MICROPLANE

2 TEASPOONS SUGAR

1 TEASPOON SALT

1/4 TEASPOON GROUND WHITE PEPPER

2 TABLESPOONS SOY SAUCE

1 TABLESPOON SHAOXING WINE (SEE PANTRY, P. 19)

2 TEASPOONS RICE VINEGAR

1 CUP CONCENTRATED AND CHILLED CHICKEN STOCK (P. 87)

DOUGH FROM BAOZI (P. 123), RISEN BUT NOT PORTIONED

PLACE THE PORK, GREEN ONIONS, GINGER, GARLIC, SUGAR, SALT, WHITE PEPPER, SOY SAUCE, WINE, AND VINEGAR IN A MEDIUM BOWL.

USE YOUR HAND TO VIGOROUSLY MIX UNTIL THOROUGHLY COMBINED, 20 TO 30 SECONDS.

THESE CRISPY PAN-FRIED BAOZI HAIL FROM SHANGHAI, WHERE THEY ARE COMMONLY EATEN IN THE MORNING FOR BREAKFAST.

LIKE MOST DUMPLINGS, THEY CAN RANGE IN SIZE AND FILLING, BUT WE LIKE TO MAKE THEM ABOUT HALF THE SIZE OF OUR OTHER BAOZI AND FILL THEM WITH GROUND PORK AND A BIT OF THE GELATINOUS CHICKEN STOCK USED IN XIAOLONGBAO (P. 83).

THEN "KNEAD" THE FILLING BY FOLDING IT OVER ON ITSELF REPEATEDLY FOR ANOTHER 90 SECONDS.

FINISH EMULSIFYING THE FILLING BY CONTINUOUSLY PICKING IT UP AND SLAPPING IT BACK DOWN INTO THE BOWL FOR ANOTHER 30 SECONDS.

TO TRY THE FILLING, MICROWAVE ABOUT A TEASPOON OF IT FOR 20 TO 30 SECONDS AND ADJUST THE SEASONING TO TASTE.

ADD THE CHILLED CHICKEN STOCK AND MIX WELL WITH A SPOON UNTIL INCORPORATED.

REFRIGERATE THE MIXTURE FOR AT LEAST 1 HOUR BEFORE FILLING THE DOUGH,

OR FREEZE IN AN AIRTIGHT CONTAINER FOR UP TO 1 MONTH.

TO FILL AND FOLD SHENG JIAN BAOZI, PLACE HALF OF THE RISEN DOUGH BALL ON A LIGHTLY FLOURED SURFACE

AND USE YOUR HANDS TO ROLL IT INTO A LOG ABOUT 1 FOOT LONG.

CUT THE LOG IN HALF,

AND THEN CUT EACH HALF IN HALF SO YOU HAVE FOUR PIECES.

CUT EACH OF THESE PIECES INTO FOUR EQUAL PARTS AGAIN.

THEN REPEAT THE PROCESS WITH THE RESERVED HALF OF DOUGH SO YOU HAVE 32 EQUAL PIECES IN TOTAL.

SET EACH DOUGH PIECE ON ITS CUT SIDE, GIVE IT A LITTLE PINCH TO SHAPE IT INTO A DISC,

AND FLATTEN IT AS MUCH AS POSSIBLE WITH THE HEEL OF YOUR HAND.

USING A SMALL WOODEN DOWEL (SEE EQUIPMENT, P. 20) OR A ROLLING PIN ON A LIGHTLY FLOURED SURFACE, ROLL EACH PIECE OF DOUGH INTO A ROUND MEASURING ABOUT 2½ TO 3 INCHES IN DIAMETER.

LINE A BAKING SHEET WITH PARCHMENT PAPER.

WORKING IN BATCHES (IT IS VERY IMPORTANT TO KEEP THE FILLING AS COOL AS POSSIBLE!),

AND KEEP THE REST REFRIGERATED UNTIL NEEDED.

START BY PLACING ONE-THIRD OF THE FILLING IN A SMALL BOWL

PLACE ABOUT 1 TABLESPOON OF FILLING IN THE MIDDLE OF EACH PIECE OF DOUGH, LEAVING ABOUT ½ INCH OF DOUGH AROUND THE FILLING.

SHAPE USING THE MOMO TECHNIQUE (P. 42),

(P. 42),

BUT RATHER THAN SEALING WITH A PINCHED RIM, JUST FINISH BY GIVING THE TOP A LIGHT SQUEEZE AND A TWIST TO SEAL THE BAOZI COMPLETELY.

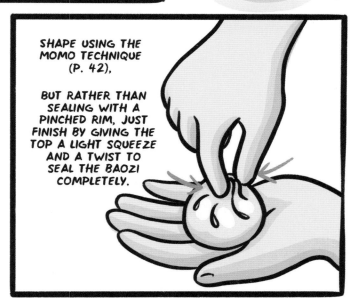

PLACE THE BAOZI ON THE BAKING SHEET, LEAVING 1 INCH AROUND EACH ONE FOR SPACE AS THEY PROOF.

145

COVER LOOSELY WITH PLASTIC WRAP

AND LET RISE IN A WARM SPOT UNTIL DOUBLED IN SIZE, ABOUT 30 MINUTES.

BAOZI ARE DIFFICULT TO PROOF AND STEAM FROM A FROZEN STATE, SO COOK IMMEDIATELY AS DIRECTED UNDER PAN-FRYING (P. 56),

AND SERVE IMMEDIATELY WITH RAYU (P. 190) OR BLACK VINEGAR DIPPING SAUCE (P. 182).

SIOPAO ASADO

INGREDIENTS:

2 TABLESPOONS NEUTRAL OIL OR LARD

2 POUNDS BONELESS PORK SHOULDER, CUT INTO 2-INCH CUBES

1 LARGE ONION, DICED

6 GARLIC CLOVES, SMASHED WITH THE SIDE OF A KNIFE

2 BAY LEAVES

1 CUP WATER

¼ CUP HOISIN SAUCE

2 TABLESPOONS SOY SAUCE

2 TABLESPOONS FISH SAUCE (SEE PANTRY, P. 18)

2 TABLESPOONS RICE VINEGAR

2 TABLESPOONS CORNSTARCH MIXED WITH 2 TABLESPOONS WATER

DOUGH FROM BAOZI (P. 123)

HEAT A HEAVY, LIDDED DUTCH OVEN OVER MEDIUM-HIGH HEAT AND ADD THE OIL.

ADD THE PORK AND SEAR ON THREE SIDES, 2 TO 3 MINUTES PER SIDE.

THESE FILIPINO BUNS ARE FILLED WITH RICH, GARLICKY, TENDER BRAISED PORK.

WE LIKE PORK SHOULDER (ALSO CALLED PORK BUTT) FOR ITS DELECTABLE, UNCTUOUS QUALITY — JUST BE SURE TO COOK IT LONG ENOUGH THAT ALL THE GELATIN AND COLLAGEN BREAKS DOWN FOR MAXIMUM, MELTY MOUTHFEEL POTENTIAL.

ADD THE ONION AND GARLIC AND COOK FOR ANOTHER 3 MINUTES, STIRRING FREQUENTLY.

ADD THE BAY LEAVES, WATER, HOISIN SAUCE, SOY SAUCE, FISH SAUCE, AND VINEGAR,

STIR WELL, AND BRING TO A SIMMER.

LOWER THE HEAT TO MAINTAIN A SIMMER AND COVER.

COOK UNTIL MEAT IS TENDER AND FALLING APART AND A CHOPSTICK CAN EASILY BE INSERTED INTO A PIECE (AN INTERNAL TEMPERATURE OF ABOUT 190°F), ABOUT 1 HOUR.

UNCOVER AND REMOVE THE BAY LEAVES.

KEEP AT A SIMMER AND STIR IN THE CORNSTARCH-WATER MIXTURE.

COOK UNTIL THICKENED, 1 TO 2 MINUTES.

REMOVE FROM THE HEAT AND LET SIT UNTIL COOL ENOUGH TO HANDLE.

USE TWO FORKS TO SHRED THE PORK AND MASH THE GARLIC AND ONIONS IN WITH IT.

REFRIGERATE THE FILLING IN ITS COOKING LIQUID UNTIL FULLY COOL.

NOTE THAT THE LIQUID WILL SOLIDIFY AS IT COOLS — THAT'S OK, AS IT WILL TURN BACK INTO THE WARM SAUCE WHEN YOU STEAM THE BUNS, SO BE SURE TO INCLUDE IT WHEN YOU MEASURE THE FILLING!

USE 2 TABLESPOONS PER BUN AS A FILLING AS DIRECTED IN BAOZI (P. 123).

ALTERNATIVELY, STORE IN THE REFRIGERATOR FOR UP TO 5 DAYS OR FREEZE IN AN AIRTIGHT CONTAINER FOR UP TO 3 MONTHS.

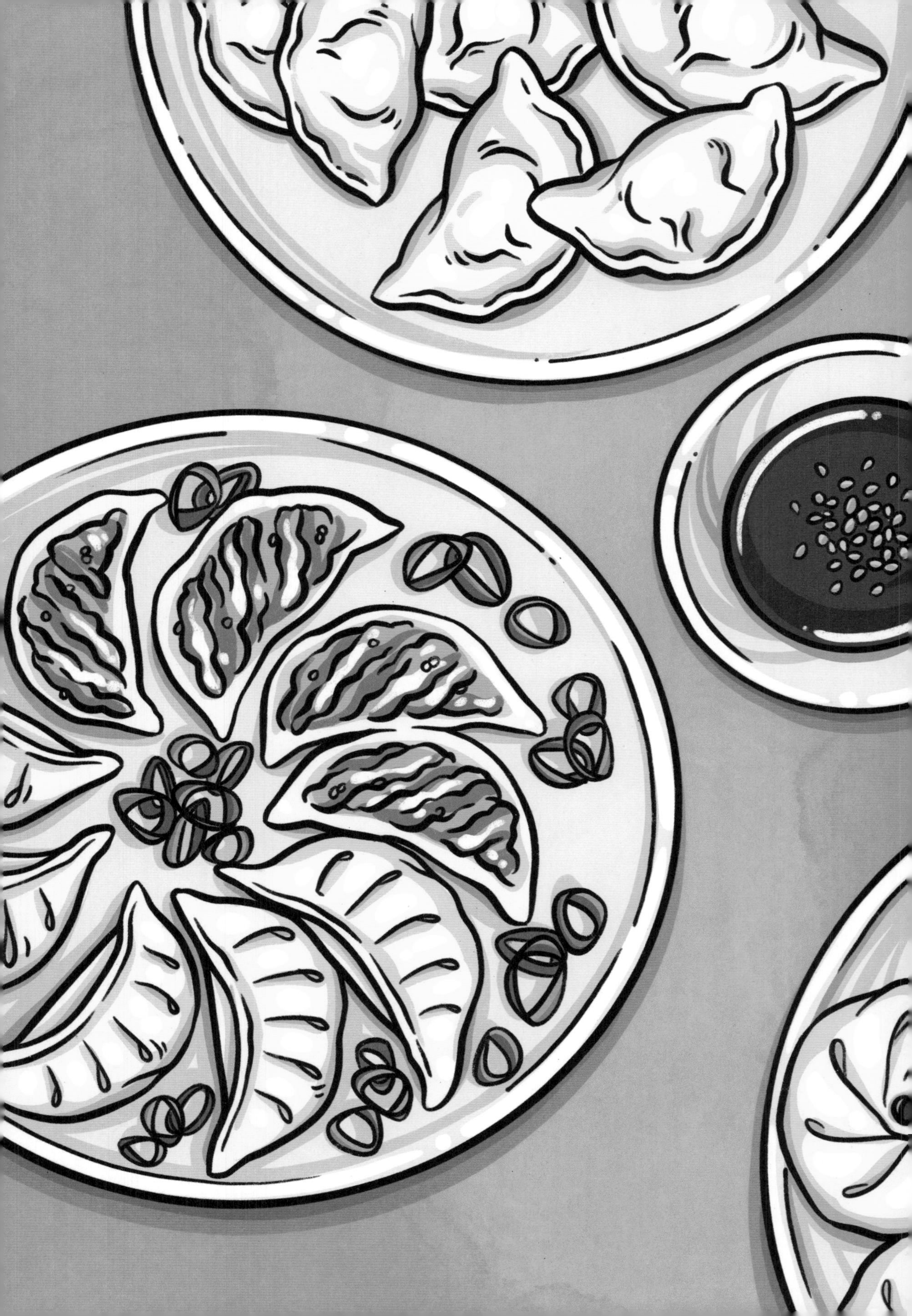

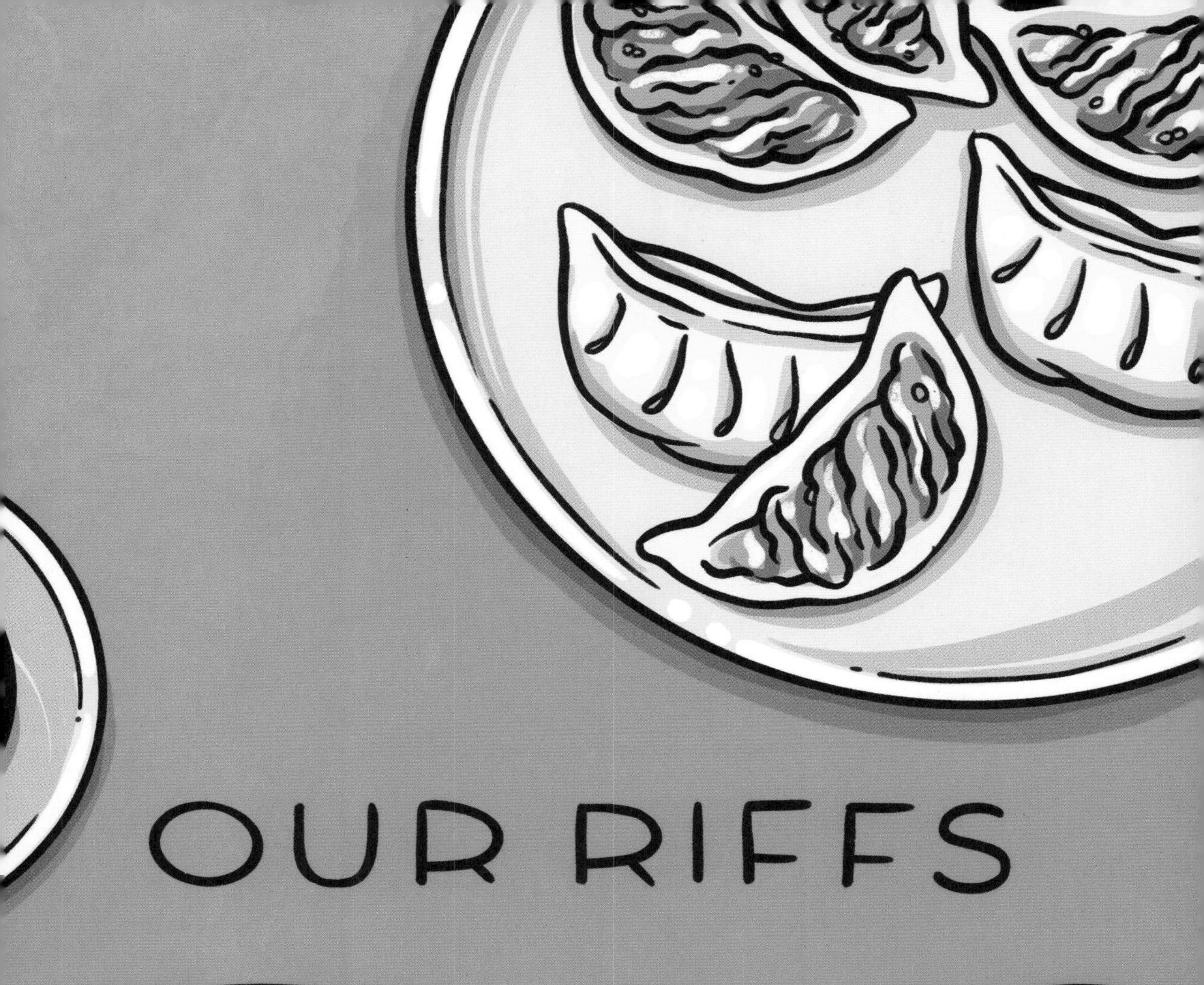

OUR RIFFS

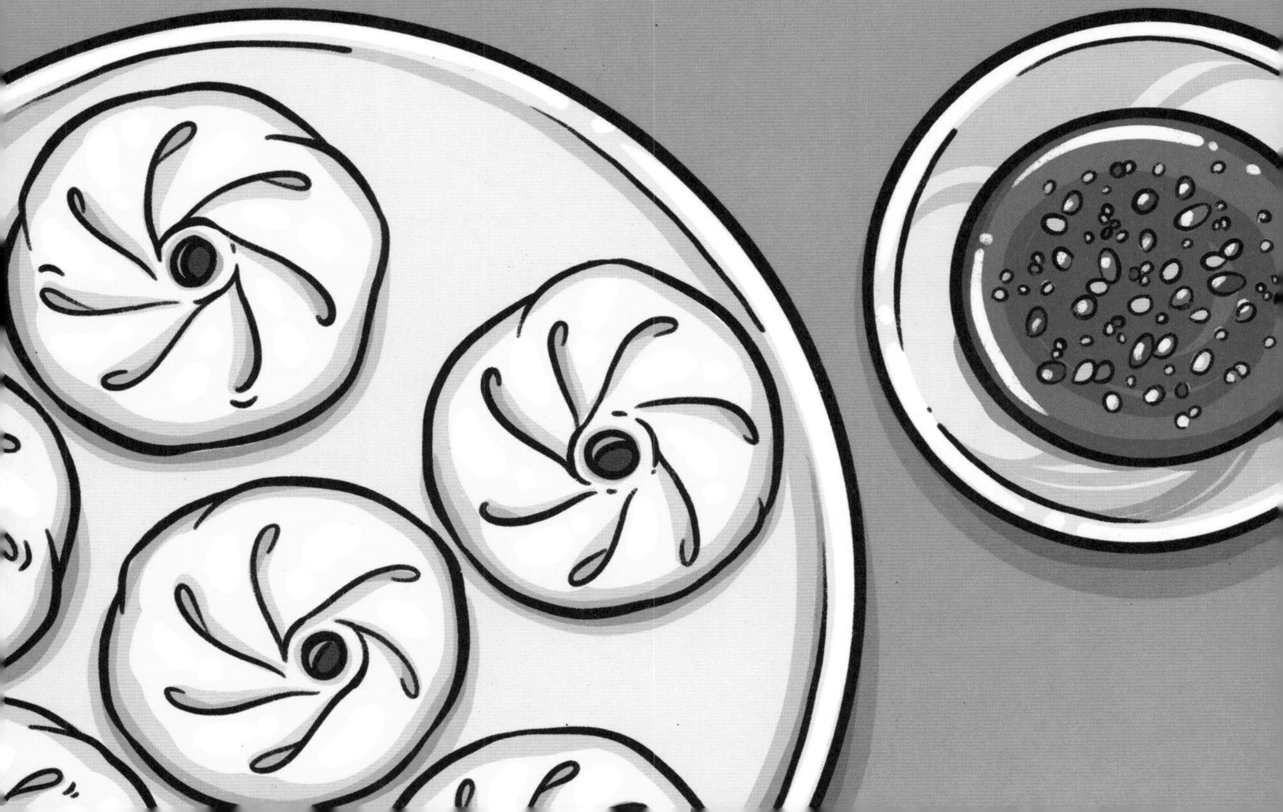

SPICY LAMB DUMPLINGS

MAKES ABOUT 48 DUMPLINGS

INGREDIENTS:

12 OUNCES GROUND LAMB

4 OUNCES GROUND BEEF

3 GARLIC CLOVES, MINCED

¼ BUNCH PARSLEY, MINCED (ABOUT 2 TABLESPOONS)

1 EGG

1 TABLESPOON GROUND CUMIN

2 TEASPOONS SALT

1 TEASPOON FRESHLY GROUND BLACK PEPPER

1 TEASPOON SUGAR

1 TEASPOON CAYENNE PEPPER, OR MORE OR LESS TO TASTE

½ TEASPOON GROUND TURMERIC

1 TABLESPOON OLIVE OIL

1 TEASPOON RICE VINEGAR

48 HOMEMADE DUMPLING WRAPPERS (P. 27) OR STORE-BOUGHT GYOZA WRAPPERS

PLACE THE LAMB, BEEF, GARLIC, PARSLEY, EGG, CUMIN, SALT, BLACK PEPPER, SUGAR, CAYENNE, TURMERIC, OLIVE OIL, AND VINEGAR IN A LARGE BOWL.

THIS IS OUR OWN LITTLE RIFF ON A TASTY LAMB-FILLED DUMPLING, ZIPPIER AND SPICIER THAN THE TRADITIONAL MONGOLIAN LAMB BUUZ (P. 118).

USE YOUR HAND TO VIGOROUSLY MIX THE FILLING UNTIL IT STARTS TO COME TOGETHER, 20 TO 30 SECONDS.

FEEL FREE TO PLAY WITH THE LAMB-TO-BEEF RATIO DEPENDING ON YOUR TASTE PREFERENCE, AND TURN THE SPICE UP WITH MORE CAYENNE IF YOU WANT MORE OF A KICK!

THEN "KNEAD" THE FILLING BY FOLDING IT OVER ON ITSELF REPEATEDLY FOR ANOTHER 90 SECONDS.

THE MIXTURE SHOULD BE COHESIVE AND WON'T NEED THE FORCEFUL SLAPPING MOTION USED IN THE WETTER PORK-BASED FILLINGS.

TO TRY THE FILLING, MICROWAVE ABOUT A TEASPOON OF IT FOR 20 TO 30 SECONDS AND ADJUST THE SEASONING TO TASTE.

THE FILLING MAY BE USED RIGHT AWAY, REFRIGERATED FOR UP TO 3 DAYS, OR FROZEN IN AN AIRTIGHT CONTAINER FOR UP TO 2 MONTHS.

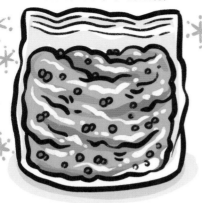

FOLD!

FILL EACH WRAPPER WITH ABOUT 2 TEASPOONS OF FILLING AND FOLD AS DESIRED — WE LIKE MOMOS (P. 42) —

COOK!

AND COOK AS DESIRED (WE SUGGEST PAN-FRYING, P. 56).

SERVE!

SERVE IMMEDIATELY WITH BURMESE GARLIC-CHILE SAUCE (P. 189).

ALTERNATIVELY, FREEZE UNCOOKED (P. 62).

SESAME CHICKEN DUMPLINGS

MAKES ABOUT 48 DUMPLINGS

INGREDIENTS:

1 POUND GROUND CHICKEN

2 GARLIC CLOVES, MINCED

2-INCH PIECE GINGER, PEELED AND GRATED ON A MICROPLANE

4 GREEN ONIONS, TRIMMED AND MINCED

1 FRESNO CHILE OR RED FINGER CHILE, STEMMED, SEEDED, AND MINCED

3 LARGE BASIL LEAVES, MINCED (ABOUT 1 TABLESPOON)

1 EGG

1 TABLESPOON TOASTED WHITE SESAME SEEDS

1½ TEASPOONS SUGAR

1 TEASPOON SALT

1 TEASPOON FRESHLY GROUND BLACK PEPPER

½ TEASPOON GROUND CUMIN

½ TEASPOON SMOKED PAPRIKA

½ TEASPOON SICHUAN PEPPERCORNS, GROUND AND SIFTED AS IN MA LA WONTONS (P. 103)

¼ TEASPOON CAYENNE PEPPER

¼ TEASPOON GROUND FENNEL SEEDS

¼ TEASPOON CHINESE FIVE-SPICE POWDER

2 TABLESPOONS TOASTED SESAME OIL

1 TEASPOON FISH SAUCE (SEE PANTRY, P. 18)

1 TEASPOON RICE VINEGAR

48 HOMEMADE DUMPLING WRAPPERS (P. 27) OR STORE-BOUGHT GYOZA WRAPPERS

NEUTRAL OIL TO FRY (OPTIONAL)

PLACE THE CHICKEN, GARLIC, GINGER, GREEN ONIONS, CHILE, BASIL, EGG, SESAME SEEDS, SUGAR, SALT, BLACK PEPPER, CUMIN, SMOKED PAPRIKA, SICHUAN PEPPERCORNS, CAYENNE, FENNEL, FIVE-SPICE POWDER, SESAME OIL, FISH SAUCE, AND VINEGAR IN A LARGE BOWL.

USE YOUR HAND TO VIGOROUSLY MIX THE FILLING UNTIL IT STARTS TO COME TOGETHER, 20 TO 30 SECONDS.

THIS RIFF PUTS ALL THE TASTY FLAVORS OF SESAME CHICKEN FROM THE CORNER TAKEOUT JOINT INTO DUMPLING FORM!

THEN "KNEAD" THE FILLING BY FOLDING IT OVER ON ITSELF REPEATEDLY FOR ANOTHER 90 SECONDS.

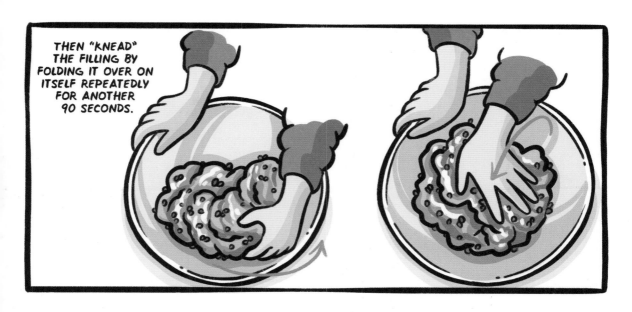

FINISH EMULSIFYING THE FILLING BY CONTINUOUSLY PICKING IT UP AND SLAPPING IT BACK DOWN INTO THE BOWL FOR ANOTHER 30 SECONDS.

THE MIXTURE SHOULD BE COHESIVE.

TO TRY THE FILLING, MICROWAVE ABOUT A TEASPOON OF IT FOR 20 TO 30 SECONDS AND ADJUST THE SEASONING TO TASTE.

THE FILLING SHOULD BE USED RIGHT AWAY OR FROZEN FOR UP TO 2 MONTHS IN AN AIRTIGHT CONTAINER.

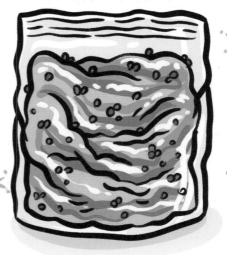

FOLD!

FILL EACH WRAPPER WITH ABOUT 2 TEASPOONS OF FILLING AND FOLD AS DESIRED — WE LIKE PLEATED CRESCENTS (P. 36) —

COOK!

AND COOK AS DESIRED (WE SUGGEST DEEP-FRYING, P. 59, OR PAN-FRYING, P. 56).

SERVE!

SERVE IMMEDIATELY WITH SWEET CHILE SAUCE (P. 186) OR SESAME-SOY DIPPING SAUCE (P. 185).

ALTERNATIVELY, FREEZE UNCOOKED (P. 62).

MAPLE, BACON & EGG DUMPLINGS

MAKES ENOUGH FILLING FOR ABOUT 12 DUMPLINGS OR 6 BAOZI

INGREDIENTS:

6 LARGE EGGS

2 TABLESPOONS MAPLE SYRUP, PLUS MORE TO SERVE (OPTIONAL)

½ TEASPOON SALT

½ TEASPOON FRESHLY GROUND BLACK PEPPER

8 OUNCES BACON, PREFERABLY THICK-CUT, CUT CROSSWISE INTO ¼-INCH LARDONS

¼ CUP WATER

3 GREEN ONIONS, TRIMMED AND MINCED

12 HOMEMADE DUMPLING WRAPPERS (P. 27) OR STORE-BOUGHT GYOZA WRAPPERS, OR DOUGH FOR 6 BAOZI (P. 123)

BEAT THE EGGS WITH THE MAPLE SYRUP, SALT, AND PEPPER AND SET ASIDE.

PLACE BACON AND WATER IN A MEDIUM SKILLET OVER HIGH HEAT.

THE WATER ALLOWS ENOUGH HEAT TO RENDER THE FAT FROM THE BACON, BUT NOT SO MUCH THAT THE BACON WILL BURN.

THIS FILLING RIFF WORKS BEST IN A BREAKFAST BAOZI, BUT WE ALSO LOVE A MESS OF MOMO-SHAPED PAN-FRIED DUMPLINGS!

AND REMEMBER: THE KEY TO A GOOD SCRAMBLED EGG IS COOKING IT LESS THAN YOU THINK YOU SHOULD — CARRYOVER HEAT WILL COOK IT THROUGH!

ONCE THE WATER EVAPORATES FROM THE PAN, LOWER THE HEAT TO LOW, AND COOK UNTIL THE BACON IS CRISPY, 5 TO 10 MINUTES.

ONCE THE WATER EVAPORATES, THE FAT WILL BE LEFT BEHIND FOR THE BACON TO CRISP UP IN.

ADD THE GREEN ONIONS AND COOK UNTIL FRAGRANT AND SOFTENED, ABOUT 90 SECONDS.

LEAVING ALL THE BACON FAT IN THE PAN, RAISE THE HEAT TO MEDIUM AND ADD THE EGG MIXTURE.

COOK, STIRRING TO SCRAMBLE THE EGGS, AND REMOVE FROM THE HEAT WHILE THE EGGS ARE STILL SOMEWHAT WET (BUT NOT RUNNY).

CONTINUE TO STIR UNTIL THE EGGS HAVE SET

AND TRANSFER TO A BOWL.

REFRIGERATE UNTIL FULLY COOL. NOTE THAT THIS FILLING WON'T FREEZE WELL!

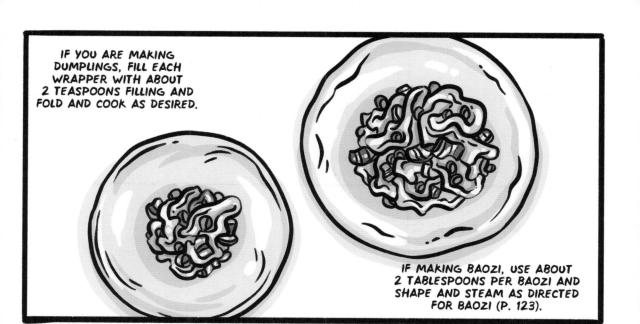

IF YOU ARE MAKING DUMPLINGS, FILL EACH WRAPPER WITH ABOUT 2 TEASPOONS FILLING AND FOLD AND COOK AS DESIRED.

IF MAKING BAOZI, USE ABOUT 2 TABLESPOONS PER BAOZI AND SHAPE AND STEAM AS DIRECTED FOR BAOZI (P. 123).

THESE ARE DELICIOUS DIPPED IN MORE MAPLE SYRUP, BUT THE SWEET CHILE SAUCE (P. 186) IS GREAT, TOO!

KALE, MUSHROOM & BUTTERNUT SQUASH DUMPLINGS

MAKES ENOUGH FILLING FOR ABOUT 48 DUMPLINGS OR 24 BAOZI

INGREDIENTS:

1 SMALL BUTTERNUT SQUASH

1 OUNCE DRIED SHIITAKE MUSHROOMS

8 OUNCES CRIMINI MUSHROOMS, FINELY CHOPPED

2 TABLESPOONS NEUTRAL OIL

1 TEASPOON SALT

2 PACKED CUPS KALE, STEMS REMOVED AND LEAVES JULIENNED (ABOUT ½ BUNCH)

3 GREEN ONIONS, TRIMMED AND MINCED

2 GARLIC CLOVES, MINCED

2-INCH PIECE GINGER, PEELED AND MINCED

1 TEASPOON FRESHLY GROUND BLACK PEPPER

1 TABLESPOON SOY SAUCE

1 TEASPOON RICE VINEGAR

48 HOMEMADE DUMPLING WRAPPERS (P. 27) OR STORE-BOUGHT GYOZA WRAPPERS, OR DOUGH FOR 24 BAOZI (P. 123)

PREHEAT THE OVEN TO 375°F.

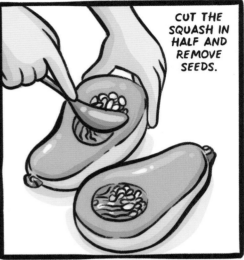

CUT THE SQUASH IN HALF AND REMOVE SEEDS.

PLACE THE SQUASH CUT-SIDE DOWN ON A PARCHMENT PAPER–LINED BAKING SHEET AND ROAST IN THE OVEN UNTIL TENDER, 45 MINUTES TO 1 HOUR.

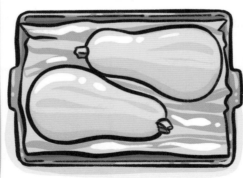

REMOVE FROM THE OVEN AND LET SIT UNTIL COOL ENOUGH TO HANDLE.

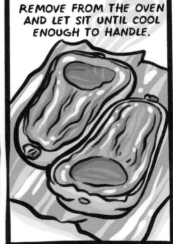

THIS VEGAN FILLING DELIVERS ON FLAVOR AND TEXTURE, WITH THE RICHNESS OF BUTTERNUT SQUASH AND THE UMAMI PRESENCE OF SHIITAKE MUSHROOMS.

USE IT TO FILL BAOZI AS DIRECTED IN BAOZI (P. 123) OR FOLD IT INTO ANY SHAPE DUMPLING YOU LIKE.

FOR DUMPLINGS, WE THINK A CRISP PAN-FRY GOES GREAT WITH THE VEGETABLE FILLINGS!

MEANWHILE, PLACE THE DRIED SHIITAKE IN A LARGE BOWL AND COVER WITH BOILING WATER.

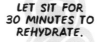

LET SIT FOR 30 MINUTES TO REHYDRATE.

DRAIN, DISCARDING THE LIQUID,

THEN FINELY CHOP THE MUSHROOMS.

COMBINE WITH THE CHOPPED CRIMINI MUSHROOMS.

HEAT A LARGE SAUTÉ PAN OVER MEDIUM-HIGH HEAT. ADD THE OIL AND SWIRL AROUND PAN,

THEN ADD THE MUSHROOMS AND SALT AND COOK, STIRRING OCCASIONALLY,

UNTIL THE MUSHROOMS ARE QUITE FRAGRANT AND MOST OF THE MOISTURE RELEASED BY THE MUSHROOMS HAS EVAPORATED, ABOUT 4 MINUTES.

ADD THE KALE, GREEN ONIONS, GARLIC, AND GINGER AND COOK, STIRRING OCCASIONALLY,

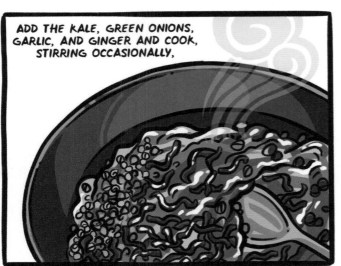

UNTIL THE KALE WILTS AND HAS REDUCED CONSIDERABLY IN VOLUME BUT IS STILL VIBRANT GREEN, ABOUT 2 MINUTES.

REMOVE FROM THE HEAT AND LET COOL SLIGHTLY,

THEN RETURN TO THE LARGE BOWL.

SCOOP THE COOLED SQUASH FLESH INTO A MEDIUM BOWL

AND MASH UNTIL SMOOTH USING A LARGE FORK (A FOOD PROCESSOR WORKS GREAT, TOO).

MEASURE OUT 1 CUP OF THE SQUASH AND ADD IT TO THE BOWL WITH THE MUSHROOMS AND KALE

(SAVE REMAINING SQUASH FOR ANOTHER USE).

ADD PEPPER, SOY SAUCE, AND VINEGAR AND MIX THOROUGHLY.

TASTE THE MIXTURE AND ADJUST THE SEASONING AS DESIRED.

AND THEN LET IT FULLY COOL.

IF YOU ARE MAKING DUMPLINGS, FILL EACH WRAPPER WITH ABOUT 2 TEASPOONS FILLING AND FOLD AS DESIRED. IF MAKING BAOZI, USE 2 TABLESPOONS FOR EACH AS DIRECTED FOR BAOZI (P. 123).

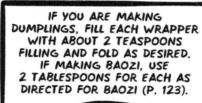

COOK AS DESIRED, OR FREEZE UNCOOKED (P. 62).

THESE FLAVORS WORK GREAT WITH SESAME-SOY DIPPING SAUCE (P. 185) AND BURMESE GARLIC-CHILE SAUCE (P. 189).

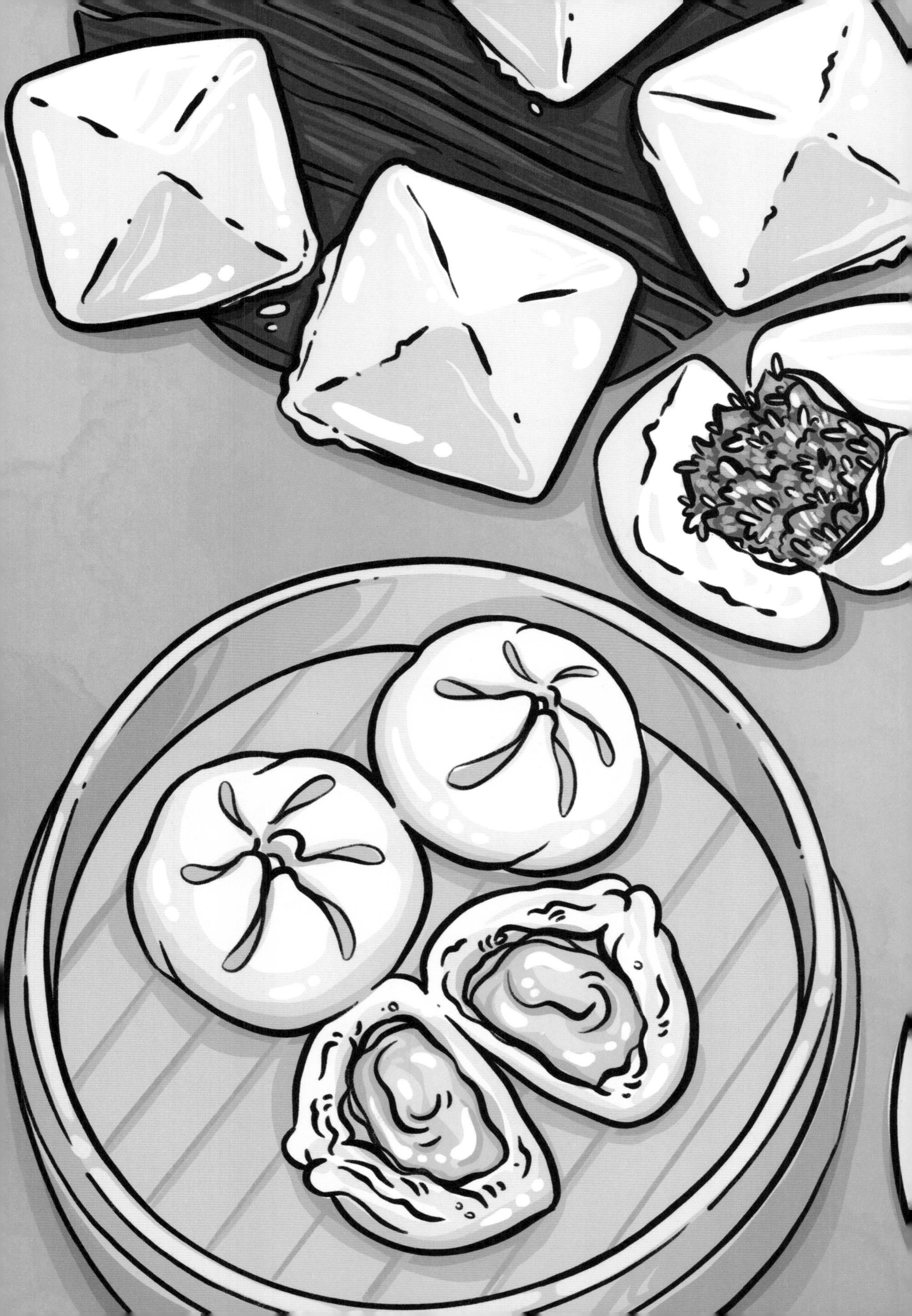

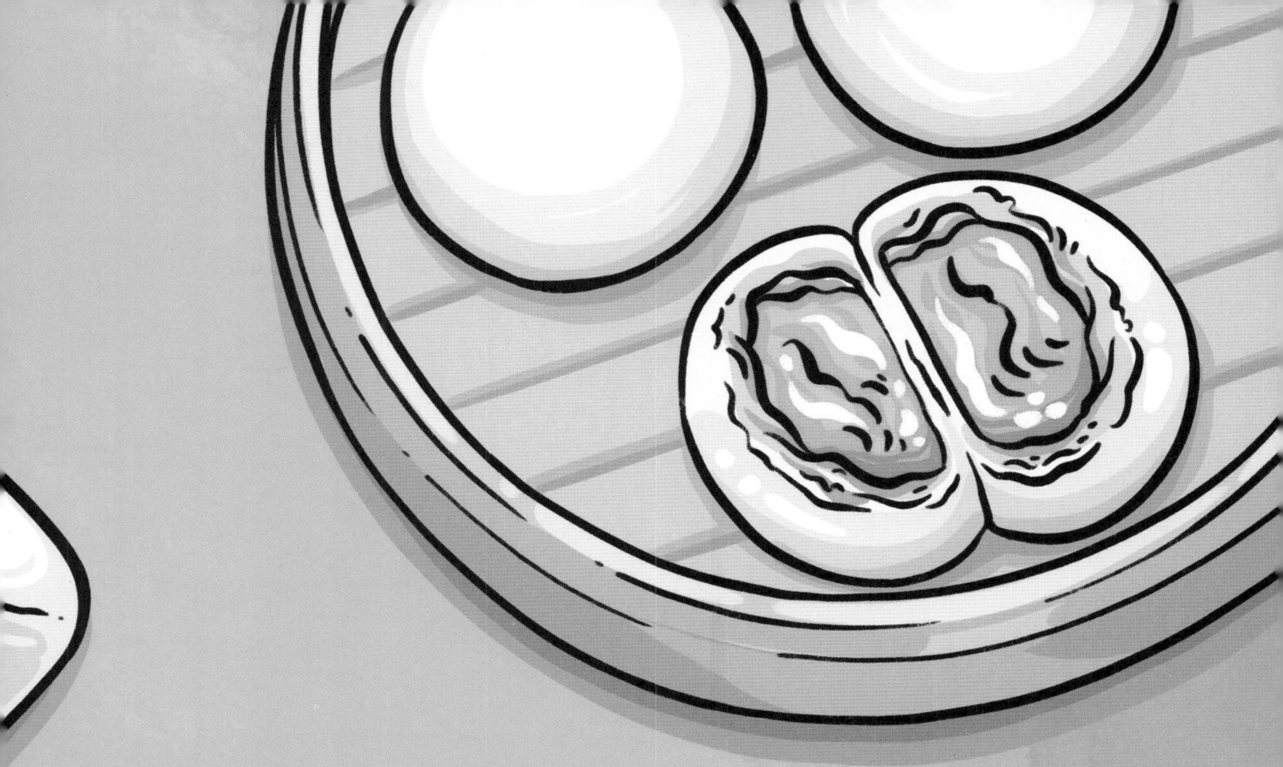

SWEET DUMPLINGS

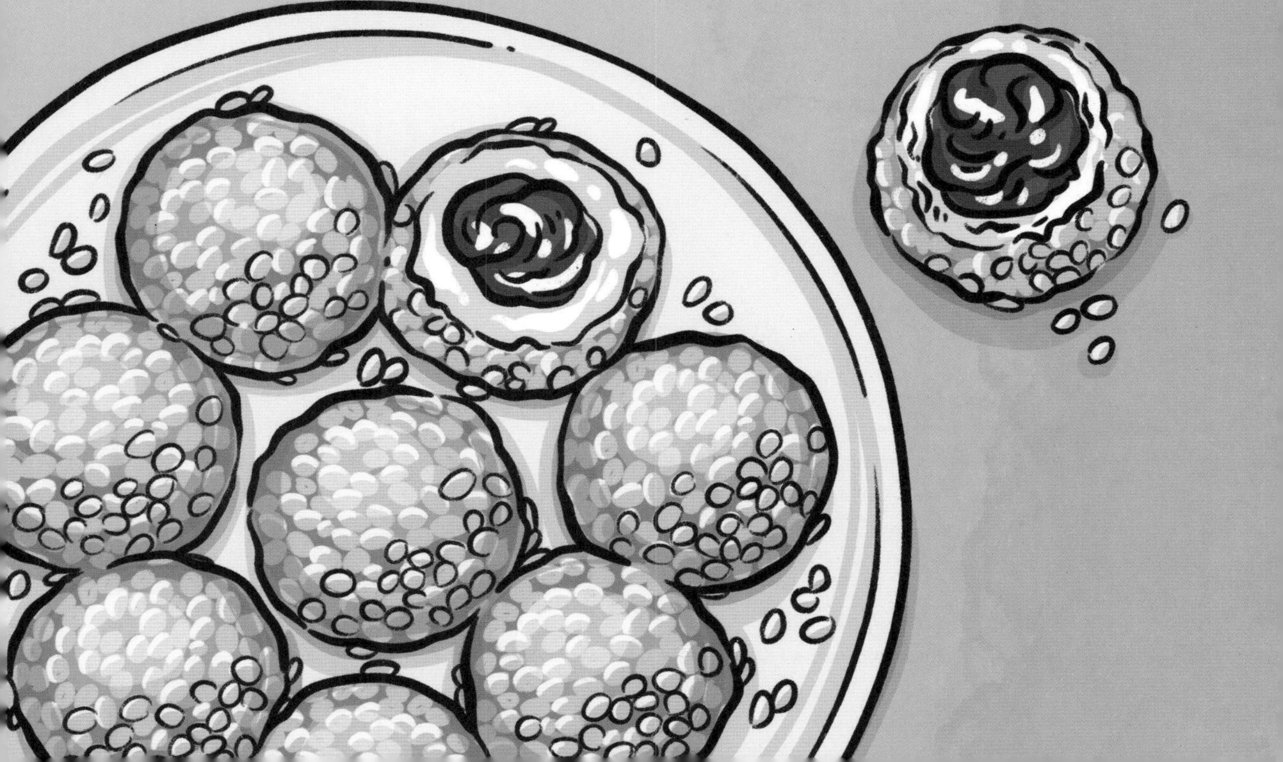

KAYA BAOZI | MALAYSIAN COCONUT JAM BAOZI

INGREDIENTS:

2 FRESH PANDAN LEAVES, ROUGHLY CHOPPED, OR 1 CUP DRIED AND TORN PANDAN LEAVES (SEE NOTE, THIS PAGE)

ONE 13.5-OUNCE CAN COCONUT MILK

½ CUP SUGAR

3 TABLESPOONS CORNSTARCH

2 EGGS

DOUGH FOR BAOZI (P. 123; SEE NOTE, P. 167), RISEN ONCE, PORTIONED, AND ROLLED

COMBINE THE PANDAN WITH THE COCONUT MILK IN A BLENDER AND PROCESS ON HIGH SPEED UNTIL WELL BLENDED, ABOUT 10 SECONDS.

THESE MALAYSIAN TREATS ARE FULL OF KAYA, A DECADENT "JAM" MADE OF COCONUT AND EGGS THAT CAN RANGE IN COLOR DEPENDING ON THE USE OF CARAMELIZED SUGAR (DARK REDDISH BROWN) OR THE ETHEREAL AND AROMATIC SOUTHEAST ASIAN PANDAN LEAF (GREEN).

STRAIN THROUGH A CHEESECLOTH-LINED FINE-MESH STRAINER INTO A SMALL SAUCEPAN, PRESSING AS MUCH LIQUID THROUGH AS POSSIBLE.

WE FAVOR THE FINESSE OF THE PANDAN LEAF VARIETY HERE. VIBRANT, FRESH PANDAN CAN BE FOUND IN ASIAN MARKETS, AND THE DRIED VARIETY IS AVAILABLE ONLINE, BUT THE AMOUNT USED MUST BE INCREASED.

ADD THE SUGAR, CORNSTARCH, AND EGGS AND WHISK TO COMBINE.

IF YOU CAN'T GET YOUR HANDS ON ANY, OMIT RATHER THAN SUBSTITUTE.

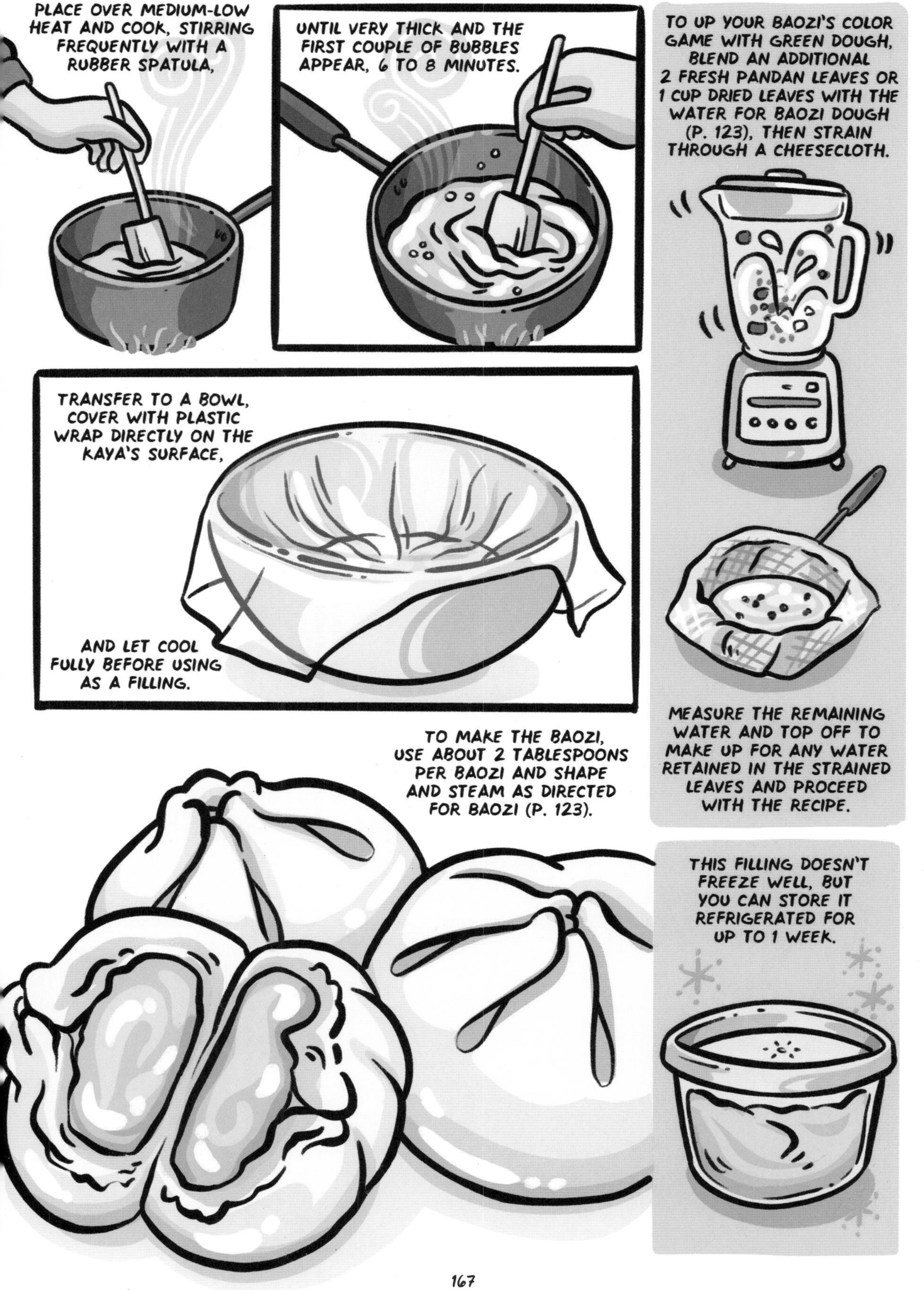
PLACE OVER MEDIUM-LOW HEAT AND COOK, STIRRING FREQUENTLY WITH A RUBBER SPATULA,
UNTIL VERY THICK AND THE FIRST COUPLE OF BUBBLES APPEAR, 6 TO 8 MINUTES.
TO UP YOUR BAOZI'S COLOR GAME WITH GREEN DOUGH, BLEND AN ADDITIONAL 2 FRESH PANDAN LEAVES OR 1 CUP DRIED LEAVES WITH THE WATER FOR BAOZI DOUGH (P. 123), THEN STRAIN THROUGH A CHEESECLOTH.
TRANSFER TO A BOWL, COVER WITH PLASTIC WRAP DIRECTLY ON THE KAYA'S SURFACE,
AND LET COOL FULLY BEFORE USING AS A FILLING.
MEASURE THE REMAINING WATER AND TOP OFF TO MAKE UP FOR ANY WATER RETAINED IN THE STRAINED LEAVES AND PROCEED WITH THE RECIPE.
TO MAKE THE BAOZI, USE ABOUT 2 TABLESPOONS PER BAOZI AND SHAPE AND STEAM AS DIRECTED FOR BAOZI (P. 123).
THIS FILLING DOESN'T FREEZE WELL, BUT YOU CAN STORE IT REFRIGERATED FOR UP TO 1 WEEK.

NAI HUANG BAOZI

CUSTARD-FILLED BAOZI

MAKES ABOUT 16 BAOZI

INGREDIENTS:

2 CUPS HALF-AND-HALF

12 TABLESPOONS SUGAR

6 LARGE EGG YOLKS

6 TABLESPOONS CORNSTARCH

4 TABLESPOONS COLD BUTTER, CUT INTO SMALL CUBES

1 TEASPOON VANILLA EXTRACT

DOUGH FOR BAOZI (P. 123; SEE NOTE, P. 170), RISEN ONCE, PORTIONED, AND ROLLED

THESE DIM SUM CLASSICS ARE FILLED WITH A FIRM EGG CUSTARD — GREAT FOR BREAKFAST OR AN AFTERNOON SNACK WITH HOT TEA!

IF YOU'VE MADE PASTRY CREAM OR PUDDING BEFORE, DON'T BE THROWN OFF BY HOW THICK THIS CUSTARD GETS — IT MAY SEEM LIKE THE EGGS ARE SCRAMBLING. JUST KEEP STIRRING UNTIL THICK AND YOU WILL END UP WITH A SMOOTH CUSTARD!

COMBINE THE HALF-AND-HALF WITH 6 TABLESPOONS OF THE SUGAR IN A SMALL SAUCEPAN AND PLACE OVER LOW HEAT.

MEANWHILE, COMBINE THE EGG YOLKS, THE REMAINING 6 TABLESPOONS SUGAR, AND THE CORNSTARCH IN A MEDIUM BOWL AND WHISK UNTIL LIGHT IN COLOR, ABOUT 1 MINUTE

(THE MIXTURE WILL BE CLUMPY AND STICKY AT FIRST, BUT WILL LOOSEN UP AS YOU WHISK IT).

WHEN THE HALF-AND-HALF BEGINS TO FORM A SKIN AND VISIBLE WISPS OF STEAM RISE FROM ITS SURFACE, REMOVE THE PAN FROM THE HEAT.

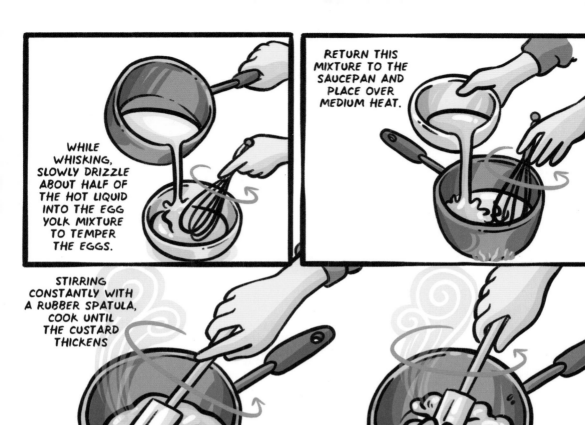

WHILE WHISKING, SLOWLY DRIZZLE ABOUT HALF OF THE HOT LIQUID INTO THE EGG YOLK MIXTURE TO TEMPER THE EGGS.

RETURN THIS MIXTURE TO THE SAUCEPAN AND PLACE OVER MEDIUM HEAT.

STIRRING CONSTANTLY WITH A RUBBER SPATULA, COOK UNTIL THE CUSTARD THICKENS

(IT WILL BECOME QUITE THICK AND ALMOST LOOK LIKE SCRAMBLED EGGS — THIS IS OKAY — JUST KEEP STIRRING!).

REMOVE FROM THE HEAT AND STIR IN THE BUTTER AND VANILLA,

USING THE FLAT SIDE OF THE SPATULA TO PRESS THE BUTTER INTO THE CUSTARD AS YOU STIR, UNTIL FULLY INCORPORATED.

TRANSFER TO A BOWL AND COVER WITH PLASTIC WRAP DIRECTLY ON THE CUSTARD TO PREVENT A SKIN FROM FORMING.

REFRIGERATE UNTIL FULLY COOL.

OUR STANDARD BAOZI DOUGH (P. 123) WILL WORK GREAT HERE, BUT YOU CAN ALSO SWEETEN THE DEAL BY REPLACING THE WATER IN THE RECIPE WITH WHOLE MILK AND UPPING THE SUGAR TO ¼ CUP, PROCEEDING AS NORMAL.

PLACE ABOUT 2 TABLESPOONS OF CUSTARD IN THE MIDDLE OF EACH PIECE OF DOUGH, LEAVING ABOUT ½ INCH OF DOUGH AROUND THE FILLING.

GATHER THE EDGES TOGETHER AND PINCH THEM TO SEAL THE BAOZI COMPLETELY.

PLACE ON INDIVIDUAL SQUARES OF PARCHMENT PAPER, SEAM-SIDE DOWN,

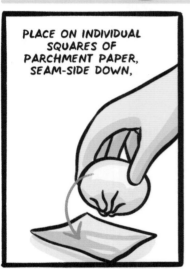

AND SET IN STEAMER BASKETS, LEAVING ABOUT 1 INCH BETWEEN THE BAOZI TO RISE AS THEY PROOF AND COOK.

ALSO NOTE THAT THIS FILLING AND SHAPING TECHNIQUE DIFFERS SLIGHTLY FROM A TYPICAL BAO.

COVER, PROOF, AND STEAM AS DIRECTED FOR BAOZI (P. 123)

AND SERVE IMMEDIATELY.

THIS FILLING DOESN'T FREEZE WELL, BUT YOU CAN STORE IT REFRIGERATED FOR UP TO 1 WEEK.

NUM KOM

SWEET CAMBODIAN RICE DUMPLINGS

MAKES ABOUT 16 NUM KOM

INGREDIENTS:

5 OUNCES UNSWEETENED SHREDDED COCONUT (ABOUT 2½ CUPS)

3 TABLESPOONS WHITE SESAME SEEDS

¼ TEASPOON SALT

1 PACKED CUP DARK BROWN SUGAR, DISSOLVED IN ½ CUP BOILING WATER

1½ CUPS GLUTINOUS RICE FLOUR (SEE PANTRY, P. 18)

¾ CUP WARM WATER

1 POUND PACKAGED BANANA LEAVES

NEUTRAL OIL FOR GREASING BANANA LEAVES

"NUM KOM," THE NAME FOR THESE CHEWY CAMBODIAN DUMPLINGS, TRANSLATES TO "RICE CAKE." THE UNSWEETENED, FRAGRANT RICE FLOUR WRAPPER IS STUFFED WITH VARIOUS SWEET FILLINGS AND CAN BE FOUND ON SPECIAL OCCASIONS.

OUR VERSION IS FRAGRANT WITH THE AROMA OF THE TOASTED COCONUT FILLING AND THE STEAMED BANANA LEAVES THEY COOK IN — WHICH ALSO SERVE AS A HANDY CARRYING CASE!

PLACE THE COCONUT IN A LARGE SKILLET AND PLACE OVER MEDIUM HEAT.

STIRRING NEARLY CONSTANTLY, COOK UNTIL AN EVEN GOLDEN BROWN, 5 TO 7 MINUTES.

ADD THE SESAME SEEDS AND SALT AND COOK FOR 1 MINUTE MORE.

CAREFULLY ADD THE BROWN SUGAR SYRUP (THE PAN WILL SIZZLE!) AND STIR UNTIL EVENLY DISTRIBUTED.

REMOVE FROM HEAT AND TRANSFER TO A MEDIUM BOWL. LET COOL COMPLETELY.

PUT THE FLOUR IN A MEDIUM BOWL AND ADD THE WATER WHILE STIRRING WITH CHOPSTICKS.

WHEN WELL COMBINED, USE YOUR HANDS TO SCRAPE THE EXCESS DOUGH FROM THE CHOPSTICKS

KEEP A SMALL BOWL OF WATER HANDY TO WET YOUR FINGERS IF THE DOUGH SHOWS ANY SIGNS OF CRACKING OR FEELS TOO DRY!

AND KNEAD THE DOUGH UNTIL IT IS SMOOTH AND PLIABLE, LIKE A SOFT MODELING CLAY.

KEEP COVERED WITH PLASTIC WRAP WHILE NOT IN USE.

PINCH OFF ENOUGH DOUGH TO FORM A BALL ABOUT 1½ INCHES IN DIAMETER.

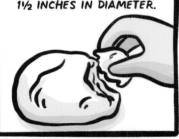

USE YOUR THUMB TO MAKE A DEEP INDENTATION IN THE BALL

AND FILL WITH ABOUT 1 TABLESPOON OF FILLING.

PINCH THE CUP CLOSED

ROLL INTO A BALL,

SET ASIDE, AND COVER WITH PLASTIC WRAP. REPEAT WITH THE REMAINING DOUGH TO FORM 16 BALLS.

LINE A STEAMER BASKET
WITH A BANANA LEAF.

CUT THE REMAINING
BANANA LEAVES INTO
8 BY 8-INCH CIRCLES.

FIND BANANA LEAVES
IN ASIAN, HISPANIC,
OR SPECIALTY MARKETS,
OR ONLINE!

FOLD ONE
IN HALF,

THEN IN
HALF AGAIN.

OPEN ONE FLAP AND
GREASE THE INSIDE
OF THE CONE WITH
A BIT OF OIL

AND PLACE A
DOUGH BALL
IN IT.

FOLD THE
FLAPS OVER

AND TUCK THE LAST
FLAP IN TO CREATE
A PYRAMID.

PLACE INTO A STEAMER BASKET POINTED-SIDE UP. REPEAT WITH THE REMAINING DOUGH BALLS AND SET ASIDE.

FILL THE BOTTOM OF YOUR STEAMER (OR A HEAVY POT OR WOK THAT YOUR BASKETS WILL FIT ON WITH JUST THE BOTTOM RIM SUBMERGED) WITH A COUPLE INCHES OF WATER AND PLACE OVER HIGH HEAT.

WHEN THE WATER IN THE STEAMER IS BOILING, CAREFULLY PLACE THE BASKET IN THE STEAMER, AND COVER WITH THE LID.

STEAM FOR 15 MINUTES, MAKING SURE THE WATER BOILS CONTINUOUSLY IN A CONTROLLED FASHION.

CAREFULLY REMOVE THE STEAMER'S LID AND CHECK ONE NUM KOM — IT SHOULD APPEAR TRANSLUCENT WHEN DONE.

SERVE IMMEDIATELY.

JIAN DUI

FRIED SESAME BALLS

MAKES ABOUT 16 JIAN DUI

INGREDIENTS:

1½ CUPS GLUTINOUS RICE FLOUR (SEE PANTRY, P. 18)

½ CUP WATER

½ PACKED CUP DARK BROWN SUGAR

¾ CUP LOTUS SEED PASTE OR SWEET RED BEAN PASTE

½ CUP WHITE SESAME SEEDS

NEUTRAL OIL FOR FRYING

PLACE THE RICE FLOUR IN A MEDIUM BOWL.

THESE DEEP-FRIED CHINESE SESAME BALLS DEVELOP A THIN, CRISPY CRUST THAT YIELDS TO A SATISFYING CHEWY DOUGH AND RICHLY SWEET PASTE (USUALLY LOTUS SEED OR RED BEAN PASTE).

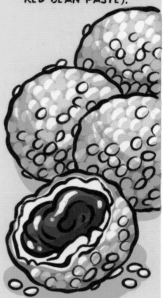

LOTUS SEED PASTE AND RED BEAN PASTE ARE COOKED, SWEETENED, AND MASHED PASTES USED WIDELY IN ASIAN DESSERTS. FIND THEM IN ASIAN MARKETS OR ONLINE.

BRING THE WATER TO A BOIL IN A SMALL SAUCEPAN AND ADD THE SUGAR, STIRRING UNTIL DISSOLVED.

BUT DON'T LIMIT YOUR FILLING CHOICES — WE'VE SEEN THESE WITH OTHER CREATIVE FILLINGS LIKE SALTY PEANUT BUTTER AND BLACK SESAME PASTE — SO FEEL FREE TO EXPERIMENT!

NOTE THAT THE DOUGH CAN DRY OUT QUICKLY, SO KEEP IT COVERED WITH PLASTIC WRAP WHEN NOT IN USE.

REMOVE FROM THE HEAT AND ADD TO THE FLOUR WHILE STIRRING WITH CHOPSTICKS.

WHEN WELL COMBINED, USE YOUR HANDS TO SCRAPE EXCESS DOUGH FROM THE CHOPSTICKS

KNEAD THE DOUGH IN THE BOWL UNTIL IT IS SMOOTH.

IF THE DOUGH CRACKS A LOT, IT IS TOO DRY — ADD MOISTURE BY WETTING YOUR HANDS WITH COLD WATER AND KNEADING IT INTO THE DOUGH AS A WHOLE OR EVEN WHEN IT IS CUT INTO PIECES BEFORE FILLING.

CUT THE DOUGH IN HALF AND WRAP HALF IN PLASTIC WRAP.

ROLL THE OTHER HALF INTO A LOG ABOUT 8 INCHES LONG AND 1 INCH WIDE.

CUT THIS LOG INTO EIGHT EQUAL PIECES, EACH ABOUT 1 INCH WIDE.

ROLL INTO BALLS,

SET ON A PLATE, AND COVER WITH PLASTIC WRAP.

REPEAT THE PROCESS WITH THE OTHER HALF OF THE DOUGH.

MEASURE OUT SIXTEEN BALLS OF LOTUS SEED OR SWEET RED BEAN PASTE, USING ABOUT 1 TEASPOON FOR EACH, AND SET ASIDE ON A PLATE.

WORKING WITH ONE PIECE OF DOUGH AT A TIME, USE YOUR THUMB TO FORM EACH DOUGH BALL INTO A CUP DEEP ENOUGH TO HOLD A PASTE BALL.

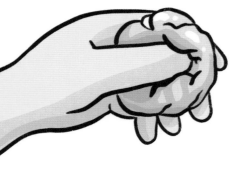

PLACE A PASTE BALL IN THE CUP

AND PINCH THE CUP CLOSED.

ROLL THE DOUGH INTO A BALL,

SET ASIDE, AND COVER WITH PLASTIC WRAP.

FILL A SMALL BOWL WITH WATER AND ANOTHER WITH THE SESAME SEEDS.

DIP A BALL IN THE WATER,

SHAKE OFF THE EXCESS,

THEN ROLL IN BOWL OF SESAME SEEDS.

ROLL IN YOUR HAND TO ENCOURAGE THE SEEDS TO STAY ADHERED TO THE BALLS.

SET ASIDE, COVER, AND REPEAT WITH THE REMAINING BALLS.

FILL A HEAVY DUTCH OVEN WITH ABOUT 2 INCHES OF OIL.

PLACE OVER MEDIUM-HIGH HEAT AND BRING THE OIL TO 350°F.

SET A COOLING RACK ON A SHEET PAN NEXT TO YOUR FRYING SETUP AND HAVE A SPIDER READY.

WORKING IN BATCHES TO ENSURE THE OIL STAYS AT 350°F, DEEP-FRY THE JIAN DUI UNTIL GOLDEN BROWN, ABOUT 3 MINUTES,

STIRRING FREQUENTLY TO PREVENT THE JIAN DUI FROM SETTLING TO THE BOTTOM OF THE POT AND BURNING.

USE THE SPIDER TO REMOVE THE JIAN DUI FROM THE OIL AND PLACE ON THE COOLING RACK.

SERVE IMMEDIATELY OR, WHEN FULLY COOLED, STORE IN A PAPER BAG FOR NO MORE THAN A DAY.

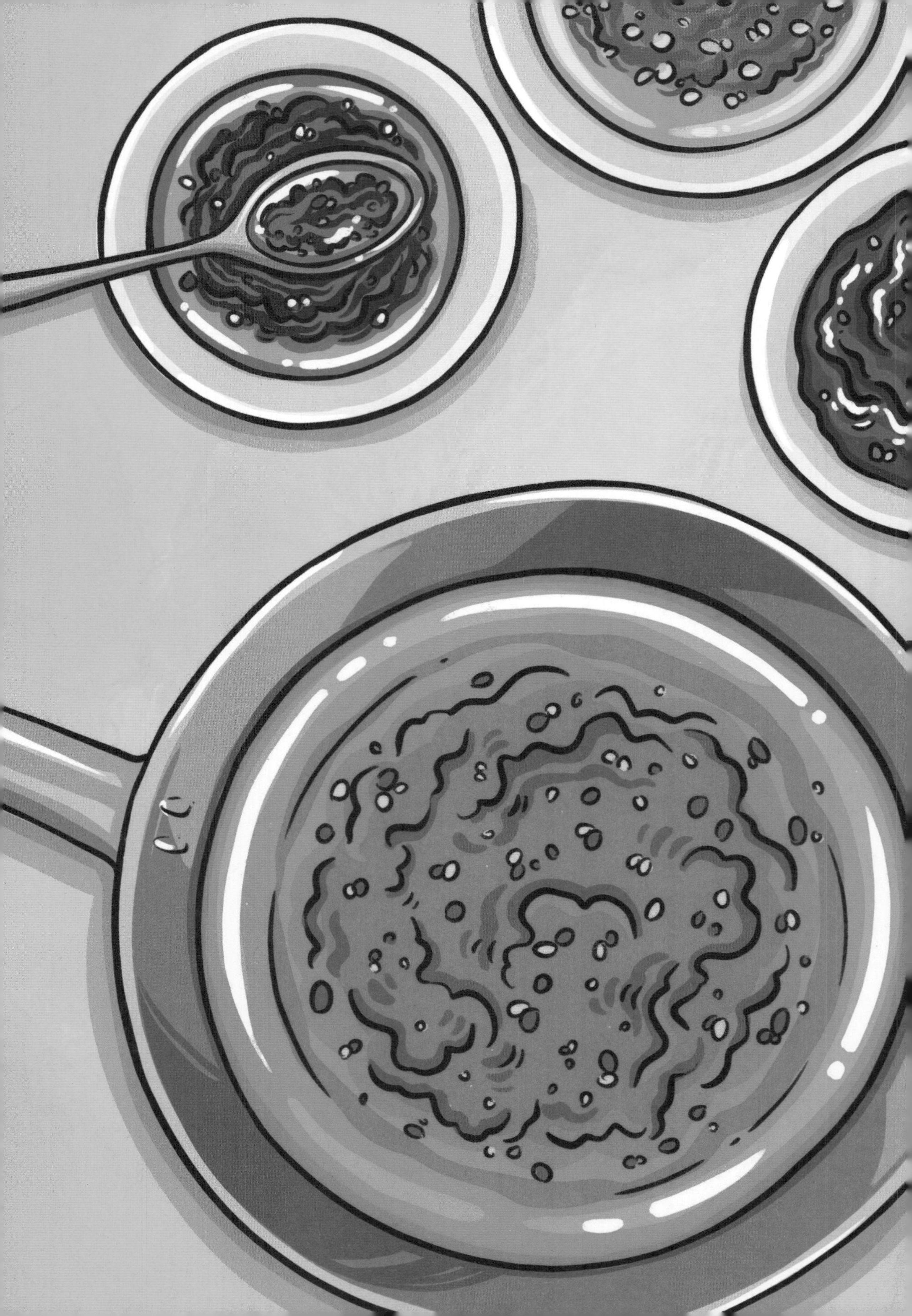

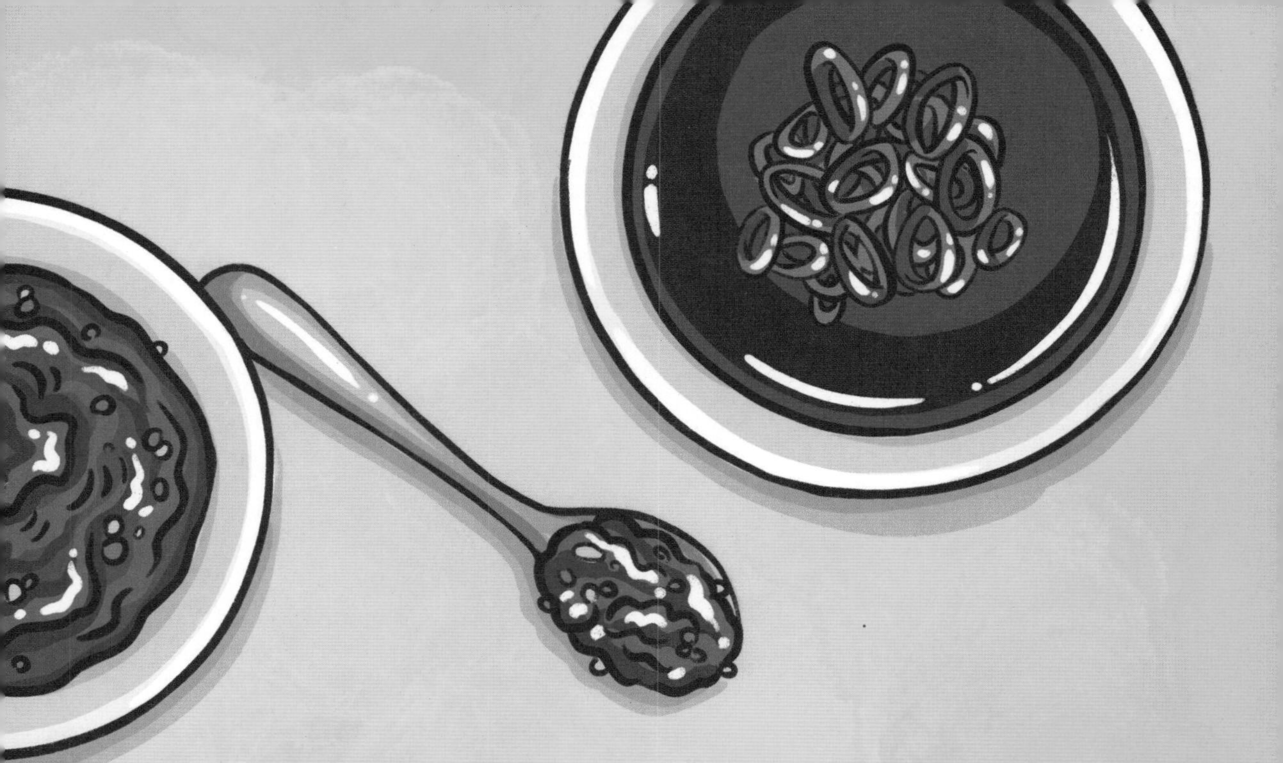

DUMPLING SAUCES

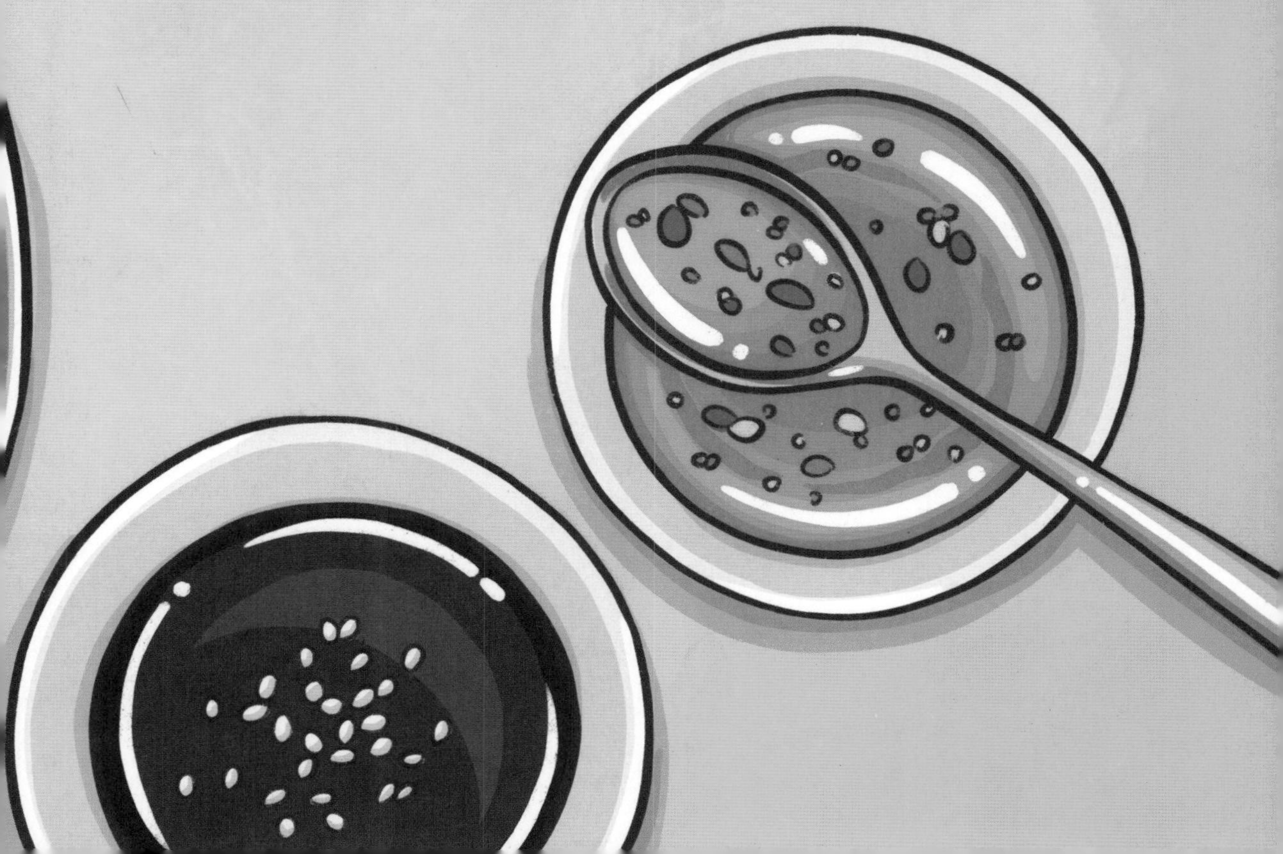

BLACK VINEGAR DIPPING SAUCE

MAKES ABOUT 1 CUP (8 SERVINGS)

INGREDIENTS:

½ CUP SOY SAUCE

¼ CUP BLACK CHINKIANG VINEGAR (SEE PANTRY, P. 18)

¼ CUP WATER

2 GARLIC CLOVES, PEELED AND GRATED ON A MICROPLANE

1-INCH PIECE GINGER, PEELED AND GRATED ON A MICROPLANE

THE MALTY, MOLASSES-LIKE DEPTH FROM THE BLACK CHINKIANG VINEGAR IN THIS TANGY DIPPING SAUCE GOES GREAT WITH THE BUTTERNUT PORK JIAOZI (P. 79).

COMBINE ALL THE INGREDIENTS IN A SMALL BOWL

AND WHISK TO COMBINE.

STORE COVERED IN THE REFRIGERATOR FOR UP TO 2 WEEKS.

GYOZA SAUCE

INGREDIENTS:

½ CUP SOY SAUCE

¼ CUP WATER

2 TABLESPOONS RICE VINEGAR

2 TABLESPOONS MIRIN (SEE PANTRY, P. 19)

1 TEASPOON TOASTED SESAME OIL

2 GREEN ONIONS, TRIMMED, WHITES MINCED AND GREENS THINLY SLICED

1 GARLIC CLOVE, PEELED AND GRATED ON A MICROPLANE

1-INCH PIECE GINGER, PEELED AND GRATED ON A MICROPLANE

THIS DIPPING SAUCE COMES TOGETHER QUICKLY AND IS THE PERFECT COMBINATION OF FRAGRANT, TANGY, AND SALTY FOR YOUR GYOZA (P. 74)!

COMBINE ALL THE INGREDIENTS IN A SMALL BOWL

AND WHISK TO COMBINE.

STORE COVERED IN THE REFRIGERATOR FOR UP TO 5 DAYS.

RAYU-KEWPIE MAYO

INGREDIENTS:

1 CUP KEWPIE MAYONNAISE

2 TABLESPOONS RAYU (P. 190) OR CHILE SAUCE OF YOUR CHOICE

THIS IS A DECADENT, SPICY SAUCE MADE WITH THE JAPANESE KEWPIE BRAND MAYONNAISE —

KEWPIE
MAYONNAISE

キユーピーマヨネーズ

A BELOVED CONDIMENT LADEN WITH DON'T-WORRY-ABOUT-IT-TOO-MUCH MSG (MONOSODIUM GLUTAMATE), WHICH ADDS A DEPTH OF UMAMI THAT REGULAR MAYONNAISE JUST CAN'T COMPETE WITH.

COMBINE THE MAYONNAISE AND RAYU IN A SMALL BOWL

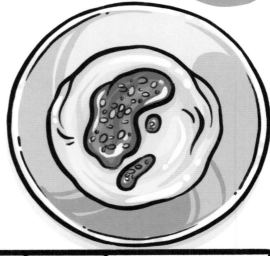

AND WHISK TO COMBINE.

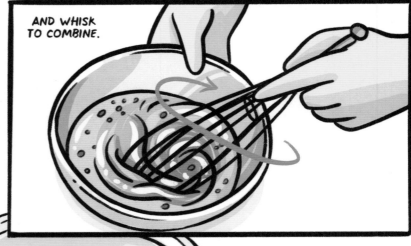

STORE COVERED IN THE REFRIGERATOR FOR UP TO 1 WEEK.

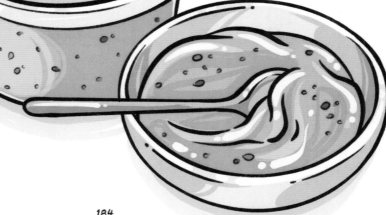

SESAME-SOY DIPPING SAUCE

MAKES ABOUT 1 CUP (8 SERVINGS)

INGREDIENTS:

⅓ CUP SOY SAUCE

¼ CUP RICE VINEGAR

¼ CUP WATER

4 TEASPOONS TOASTED SESAME OIL

2 TABLESPOONS TOASTED WHITE SESAME SEEDS

1-INCH PIECE GINGER, PEELED AND GRATED ON A MICROPLANE

COMBINE ALL THE INGREDIENTS IN A SMALL BOWL AND WHISK TO COMBINE.

BE SURE TO STIR WELL BEFORE SERVING, AS THE SESAME OIL WILL NATURALLY SEPARATE TO THE TOP OF THE SAUCE.

THIS SAUCE IS A LOW-KEY COUNTERPART TO THE BLACK VINEGAR DIPPING SAUCE (P. 182),

STORE COVERED IN THE REFRIGERATOR FOR UP TO 2 WEEKS.

WITH ROUNDER, NUTTIER NOTES FROM THE SESAME OIL, BUT PLENTY OF ACID TO CUT THE RICHNESS OF MOST OF THE DUMPLINGS IN THIS BOOK.

SWEET CHILE SAUCE

INGREDIENTS:

1 CUP WATER

1 CUP RICE VINEGAR

1 TEASPOON FISH SAUCE (SEE PANTRY, P. 18) (OPTIONAL; ADD AN EXTRA ½ TEASPOON SALT IF NOT USING)

6 GARLIC CLOVES, MINCED

4 FRESNO OR RED SERRANO CHILES, STEMMED AND MINCED (INCLUDING SEEDS), OR MORE OR LESS TO TASTE

2-INCH PIECE GINGER, PEELED AND MINCED

1 CUP SUGAR

1 TEASPOON SALT

2 TABLESPOONS CORNSTARCH WHISKED WITH ¼ CUP WATER

THIS QUICK-TO-MAKE, SWEET, TANGY, AND SPICY DIPPING SAUCE WILL GO WITH JUST ABOUT ANY DUMPLING UNDER THE SUN.

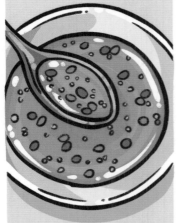

AS ALWAYS, ADJUST THE CHILE AMOUNTS TO YOUR LIKING — AND GIVE OUR FISH SAUCE UPGRADE A TRY FOR A NON-FISHY UMAMI BOOST!

PLACE THE WATER, VINEGAR, FISH SAUCE (IF USING), GARLIC, CHILES, GINGER, SUGAR, AND SALT IN A SMALL SAUCEPAN

AND BRING TO A SIMMER OVER MEDIUM-HIGH HEAT.

LOWER THE HEAT TO MAINTAIN A SIMMER AND COOK UNTIL THE RAWNESS HAS COOKED OUT OF THE GARLIC, ABOUT 2 MINUTES,

THEN WHISK IN ABOUT HALF OF THE CORNSTARCH AND WATER MIXTURE.

BRING BACK TO A SIMMER AND WHISK UNTIL THICKENED, 1 TO 2 MINUTES.

IF A THICKER SAUCE IS DESIRED, ADD THE REMAINING CORNSTARCH-WATER MIXTURE AND SIMMER UNTIL THICKENED.

REMOVE FROM THE HEAT AND LET COOL.

STIR WELL AND BRING TO ROOM TEMPERATURE BEFORE SERVING,

OR STORE COVERED IN THE REFRIGERATOR FOR UP TO 1 MONTH.

DUCK SAUCE

MAKES ABOUT 1 CUP (8 SERVINGS)

INGREDIENTS:

1 CUP APRICOT JAM

2 TABLESPOONS RICE VINEGAR

1 TEASPOON SOY SAUCE

2 GARLIC CLOVES, PEELED AND GRATED ON A MICROPLANE

1-INCH PIECE GINGER, PEELED AND GRATED ON A MICROPLANE

¼ TEASPOON CAYENNE PEPPER

PLACE ALL THE INGREDIENTS IN A SMALL SAUCEPAN OVER LOW HEAT

AND WHISK UNTIL SIMMERING.

REMOVE FROM THE HEAT AND LET COOL.

THERE ISN'T ANY DUCK IN THIS SAUCE — BUT IT SURE GOES GREAT AS A GLAZE FOR ANY ROASTED POULTRY!

SERVE IMMEDIATELY OR STORE COVERED IN THE REFRIGERATOR FOR UP TO 1 MONTH.

WE'LL SAVE THOSE SPECIFICS FOR ANOTHER COOKBOOK. FOR NOW, USE THIS SAUCE FOR DIPPING DUMPLINGS SUCH AS CRAB RANGOON (P. 112) AND ANYTHING FRIED!

BURMESE GARLIC-CHILE SAUCE

MAKES ABOUT 1 CUP (8 SERVINGS)

INGREDIENTS:

⅓ CUP ARBOL CHILES

¼ CUP WATER

8 GARLIC CLOVES, PEELED

¼ CUP RICE VINEGAR

3 TABLESPOONS FISH SAUCE (SEE PANTRY, P. 18)

1 TABLESPOON SUGAR

COMBINE THE CHILES AND WATER IN A SMALL SAUCEPAN AND BRING TO A BOIL.

LOWER THE HEAT TO MAINTAIN A SIMMER AND COOK FOR 3 MINUTES, THEN ADD THE GARLIC AND REMOVE THE PAN FROM THE HEAT.

LET SIT FOR 5 MINUTES,

THEN TRANSFER TO A BLENDER. ADD THE VINEGAR, FISH SAUCE, AND SUGAR

THIS SAUCE, ADAPTED FROM NAOMI DUGUID'S WONDERFUL COOKBOOK BURMA: RIVERS OF FLAVOR, HAS BECOME A STAPLE IN OUR PANTRIES DUE TO ITS INCREDIBLY FLAVORFUL DELIVERY OF A WALLOP OF HEAT!

AND PUREE TO THE DESIRED CONSISTENCY (WE LIKE IT NICE AND SMOOTH).

SERVE IMMEDIATELY OR STORE COVERED IN THE REFRIGERATOR FOR UP TO 1 MONTH.

RAYU

JAPANESE CHILE OIL

INGREDIENTS:

½ CUP NEUTRAL OIL

6 GARLIC CLOVES, MINCED

3-INCH PIECE OF GINGER, PEELED AND MINCED

WHITES OF 3 GREEN ONIONS, TRIMMED AND MINCED

1 TABLESPOON SHICHIMI TOGARASHI

1 TEASPOON CRUSHED RED PEPPER FLAKES

½ CUP TOASTED SESAME OIL

COMBINE THE NEUTRAL OIL, GARLIC, GINGER, AND GREEN ONIONS IN A SMALL SAUCEPAN OVER MEDIUM HEAT.

THIS JAPANESE CHILE OIL IS MADE SPICY WITH DRIED RED PEPPER FLAKES AND THE JAPANESE CHILE-BASED SPICE BLEND SHICHIMI TOGARASHI.

IT IS GREAT ON ITS OWN FOR DIPPING SOLO, DRIZZLING OVER MA LA WONTONS (P. 103), OR EVEN STIRRED INTO KEWPIE MAYONNAISE FOR A ZIPPY, CREAMY DUMPLING DUNK!

BRING TO A SIMMER AND COOK UNTIL THE VEGETABLES ARE FRAGRANT BUT NOT BROWNED, ABOUT 5 MINUTES, STIRRING OCCASIONALLY.

REMOVE FROM THE HEAT AND STIR IN SHICHIMI TOGARASHI, RED PEPPER FLAKES, AND SESAME OIL.

LET COOL.

SERVE IMMEDIATELY OR STORE COVERED IN THE REFRIGERATOR FOR UP TO 1 MONTH.

TIBETAN SEPEN

SPICY CHILE SAUCE

INGREDIENTS:

2 TABLESPOONS NEUTRAL OIL

1 MEDIUM ONION, FINELY DICED

2 TO 4 JALAPEÑOS, STEMMED, SEEDED, AND COARSELY CHOPPED, OR 2 TO 4 DRIED ARBOL CHILES, OR A COMBINATION, OR MORE OR LESS TO TASTE

2 STALKS CELERY, FINELY DICED

4 GARLIC CLOVES, THINLY SLICED

3-INCH PIECE GINGER, PEELED AND MINCED

1½ TEASPOONS SALT, PLUS MORE

2 POUNDS RIPE TOMATOES, DICED, OR ONE 28-OUNCE CAN WHOLE PEELED TOMATOES

1 TEASPOON SUGAR

2 TEASPOONS RICE VINEGAR

1 BUNCH CILANTRO, STEMS INCLUDED, COARSELY CHOPPED

HEAT A HEAVY MEDIUM SAUCEPAN OVER MEDIUM HEAT AND ADD THE OIL.

ADD THE ONION, JALAPEÑOS (IF USING DRIED ARBOLS, WAIT TO ADD), CELERY, GARLIC, GINGER, AND SALT. COOK UNTIL THE VEGETABLES ARE VIBRANT AND SOFTENED, 3 TO 5 MINUTES, STIRRING OCCASIONALLY.

THIS SPICY TIBETAN DIPPING SAUCE GOES GREAT WITH TIBETAN BEEF MOMOS (P. 115), BUT ITS AROMATIC TOMATO AND HERB FLAVOR ALSO WORKS WITH ANY OTHER DUMPLING YOU LIKE.

PLAY WITH THE HEAT LEVEL AND ADJUST THE TYPES AND AMOUNTS OF CHILES THAT YOU USE — JALAPEÑOS OFFER A FRESHER, MORE VEGETAL TASTE, DRIED ARBOLS PROVIDE STRAIGHT HEAT POWER, OR USE A COMBINATION OF BOTH!

IF YOU ARE USING DRIED ARBOLS, ADD THEM AT THIS POINT WITH THE TOMATOES, SUGAR, AND VINEGAR, BREAKING THE TOMATOES DOWN WITH A SPOON.

LOWER THE HEAT TO MAINTAIN A SIMMER AND COOK UNTIL THE WATER CONTENT REDUCES AND THE SAUCE THICKENS SLIGHTLY, ABOUT 15 MINUTES.

BE SURE TO COOK THE SAUCE DOWN A BIT, ADJUSTING FOR THE WATER CONTENT OF THE TOMATOES — WE PREFER THE SAUCE TO BE ON THE THICKER SIDE FOR EASY DIPPING. USE A FOOD PROCESSOR FOR A CHUNKY SAUCE, OR A BLENDER FOR A SMOOTH ONE!

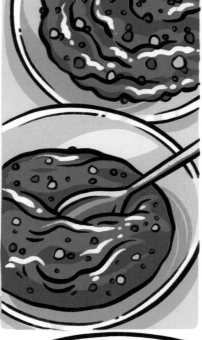

REMOVE FROM THE HEAT, ADD THE CILANTRO, AND ALLOW TO COOL SLIGHTLY.

TRANSFER TO A FOOD PROCESSOR OR BLENDER AND PUREE TO A DESIRED CONSISTENCY.

TASTE, ADJUST THE SEASONING, AND SERVE IMMEDIATELY

OR STORE COVERED IN THE REFRIGERATOR FOR UP TO 5 DAYS.

FRIED GARLIC OIL

MAKES ABOUT 1 CUP (8 SERVINGS)

INGREDIENTS:

½ CUP NEUTRAL OIL

1 HEAD GARLIC, PEELED AND MINCED

2 TABLESPOONS SOY SAUCE

1 TABLESPOON BLACK CHINKIANG VINEGAR (SEE PANTRY, P. 18)

THIS AROMATIC FRIED GARLIC OIL GETS A KICK OF ACIDITY AND MOLASSES DEPTH FROM THE BLACK VINEGAR —

A RICH, GARLICKY UPGRADE FOR STEAMED AND BOILED DUMPLINGS!

HEAT A SMALL SAUCEPAN OVER LOW HEAT AND ADD THE OIL.

ADD THE GARLIC AND COOK SLOWLY, STEEPING THE GARLIC IN THE OIL, STIRRING OCCASIONALLY, FOR 20 TO 30 MINUTES, UNTIL THE GARLIC BEGINS TO BROWN.

STIR CONSTANTLY FOR 2 TO 5 MINUTES MORE, UNTIL THE GARLIC IS A NICE, LIGHT, EVEN BROWN,

THEN REMOVE FROM HEAT AND LET COOL TO ROOM TEMPERATURE.

STIR IN THE SOY SAUCE AND VINEGAR.

BE SURE TO LET THIS OIL COME TO ROOM TEMPERATURE AND STIR WELL BEFORE SERVING.

STORE COVERED IN THE REFRIGERATOR FOR UP TO 1 MONTH.

THAT'S A WRAP!

DUMPLINGS NEEDN'T BE DAUNTING!

WE HOPE THIS BOOK HAS TAUGHT YOU THAT WITH JUST A FEW INGREDIENTS —

A WORLD OF FLAVORS AND TEXTURES CAN BE WRAPPED UP IN PLUMP LITTLE PACKETS OF DELICIOUSNESS.

AND WITH A BIT OF PLANNING AND ORGANIZATION,

YOU CAN TURN YOUR HOME KITCHEN INTO A DUMPLING FACTORY,

WHETHER IT'S FOR DINNER ONE NIGHT,

OR TO FILL A FREEZER FOR FUTURE HUNGRY DAYS!

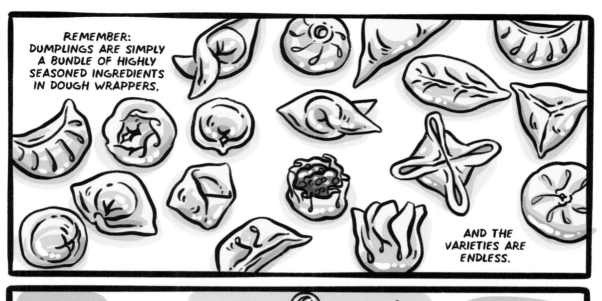

REMEMBER: DUMPLINGS ARE SIMPLY A BUNDLE OF HIGHLY SEASONED INGREDIENTS IN DOUGH WRAPPERS,

AND THE VARIETIES ARE ENDLESS.

GET CREATIVE,

THINK OF FLAVORS THAT YOU LIKE TOGETHER, AND EXPERIMENT—

CHANCES ARE, YOU'LL COME UP WITH SOME PRETTY GREAT STUFF!

AND MOST OF ALL: HAVE FUN!

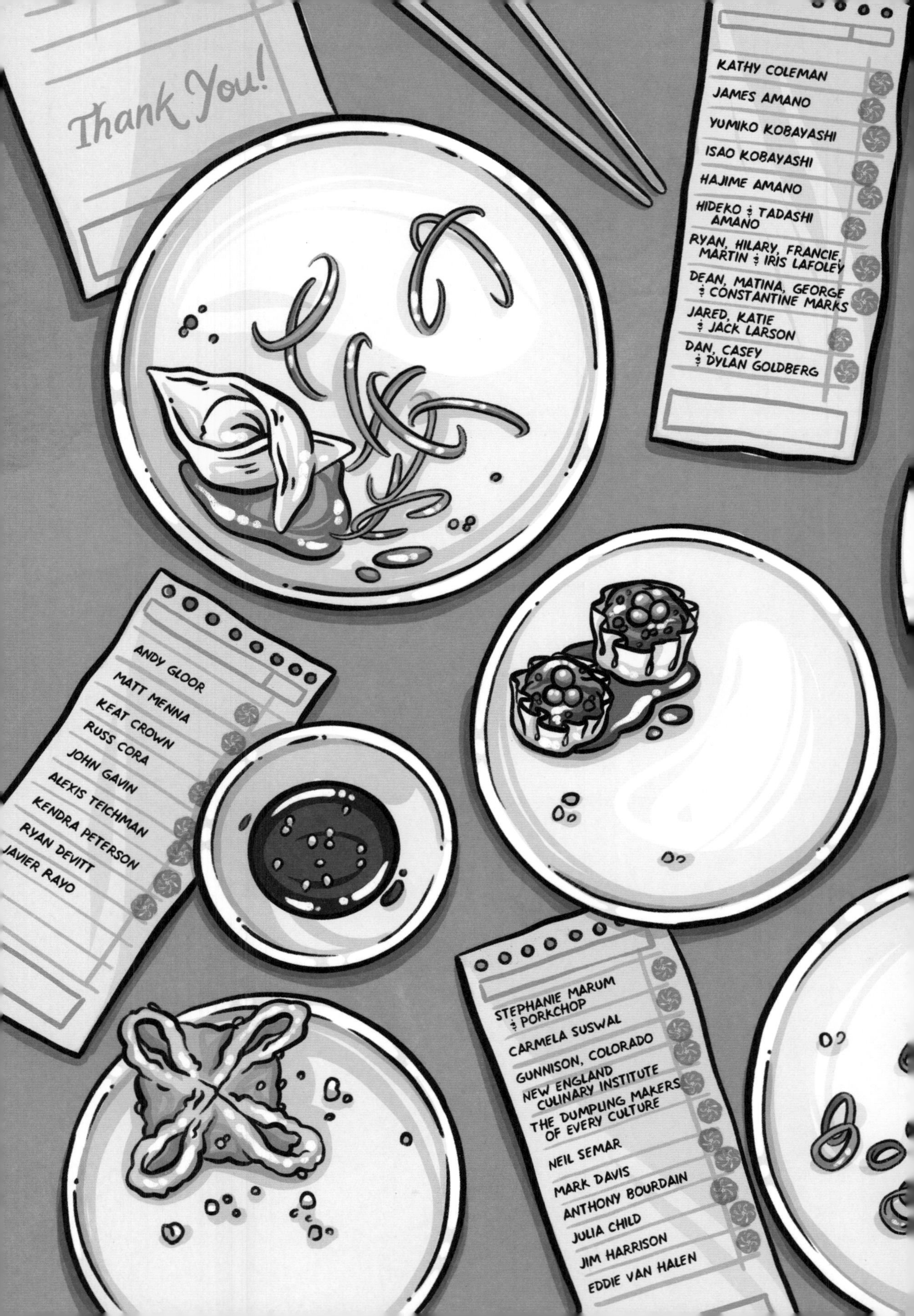

Thank You!
KATHY COLEMAN
JAMES AMANO
YUMIKO KOBAYASHI
ISAO KOBAYASHI
HAJIME AMANO
HIDEKO & TADASHI AMANO
RYAN, HILARY, FRANCIE, MARTIN & IRIS LAFOLEY
DEAN, MATINA, GEORGE & CONSTANTINE MARKS
JARED, KATIE & JACK LARSON
DAN, CASEY & DYLAN GOLDBERG
ANDY GLOOR
MATT MENNA
KEAT CROWN
RUSS CORA
JOHN GAVIN
ALEXIS TEICHMAN
KENDRA PETERSON
RYAN DEVITT
JAVIER RAYO
STEPHANIE MARUM & PORKCHOP
CARMELA SUSWAL
GUNNISON, COLORADO
NEW ENGLAND CULINARY INSTITUTE
THE DUMPLING MAKERS OF EVERY CULTURE
NEIL SEMAR
MARK DAVIS
ANTHONY BOURDAIN
JULIA CHILD
JIM HARRISON
EDDIE VAN HALEN

AMY COLLINS
KIMMY TEJASINDHU
CHLOE RAWLINS
NILES BARANOWSKI
TOKI ♯ MRS. CHENG
MARK BARANOWSKI
EILEEN DAILEY
BECKIE GAUTREAU
MARY CLAIRE SCHOLL

LIZ WAYNE
DENISE BREWER
CORINNE MUCHA
LUCY KNISLEY
LIZ ANNA KOZIK
THEO HAHN
ANDREW HUFF
GREGG ♯ TONYA
TOMLINSON

HUGH AMANO

HUGH'S FIRST DUMPLING MEMORIES ARE OF HIS MOTHER MAKING GYOZA FOR JAPANESE NIGHT AT A RESTAURANT IN THEIR SMALL COLORADO MOUNTAIN TOWN, LAYING EARLY CULINARY BEDROCK FOR HIS LIFE IN THE KITCHEN. HE FOUND SALT'S POWER TO DRAW MOISTURE OUT OF CABBAGE SCIENTIFICALLY INTRIGUING, THE SMOOTH EMULSION FORMED BY FORCEFULLY MIXING GROUND PORK WITH AROMATICS MAGICAL, AND THE VARIETY OF TEXTURE FROM VARIOUS COOKING METHODS ABSOLUTELY TRANSCENDENT.

HIS JOURNEY AS A LOVER OF DOUGH-ENCASED FOODS CONTINUED VIA TRAVEL: FREQUENT GYOZA FEASTS WITH FAMILY IN JAPAN, LATE-NIGHT DIM SUM IN MACAU FOLLOWING SEVERAL ROUNDS OF DRINKS WITH FRIENDS, AND BEEF-FILLED, GRAVY-COVERED CORNISH PASTIES IN MONTANA. WHEN A FRIEND'S ITALIAN MOTHER FIRST TAUGHT HIM HOW TO MAKE PASTA FOR TORTELLINI USING A ROLLING PIN AND HER WELL-WORN WOODEN BOARD, HE WAS HOOKED ON MAKING DUMPLINGS OF ALL FORMS.

HUGH LIVES IN CHICAGO WHERE THE ROSTER OF DOUGH-ENCASED FOODS RUNS DEEP (TAMALES, PIEROGIES, MOMOS, YOU NAME IT), WORKING AS A CHEF AND WRITER, AND COAUTHORING LET'S MAKE RAMEN! WITH SARAH BECAN. HE ALWAYS PUTS OUT A BIG BATCH OF GYOZA FOR HIS ANNUAL NEW YEAR'S EVE DINNER PARTY.

SARAH BECAN

SARAH BECAN HAS BEEN DRAWING COMICS ABOUT FOOD SINCE SHE CREATED THE WEBCOMIC *I THINK YOU'RE SAUCEOME* IN 2010, GOING ON TO PUBLISH WORK IN *SAVEUR, EATER, RODALE'S ORGANIC LIFE, CHICAGO'S READER,* AND *TASTING TABLE.* SHE WAS AWARDED A XERIC GRANT AND A STUMPTOWN TROPHY FOR OUTSTANDING DEBUT FOR HER FIRST GRAPHIC NOVEL, *THE COMPLETE OUIJA INTERVIEWS,* RELEASING HER SECOND GRAPHIC NOVEL *SHUTEYE* IN EARLY 2012. SHE LOVES DUMPLINGS IN ABSOLUTELY ANY FORM, AND LIVING IN CHICAGO DELIVERS ON THOSE AFFECTIONS: FROM PIEROGI AT STAROPOLSKA TO CHAR SIU BAO AT CHIU QUON BAKERY TO THE WANG MANDU AT JOONG BOO MARKET.

SARAH FEEDS HER STRONG INTEREST IN FOOD-BASED MANGA WITH WORKS SUCH AS TETSU KARIYA'S *OISHINBO,* GIDO AMAGAKURE'S *SWEETNESS & LIGHTNING,* AND FUMI YOSHINAGA'S *WHAT DID YOU EAT YESTERDAY?* AND IS FASCINATED BY THE STORIES THAT CAN BE TOLD THROUGH COOKING, CULINARY HISTORY, AND FOOD ILLUSTRATION. LATELY, SHE'S BEEN ILLUSTRATING COOKBOOKS, MOST RECENTLY *LET'S MAKE RAMEN!* WITH HUGH AMANO.

SHE LIVES IN CHICAGO WITH HER PARTNER NILES AND HER CAT TOKI, AND IF SHE HAD IT HER WAY, SHE'D DO NOTHING BUT DRAW PICTURES OF FOOD ALL DAY.

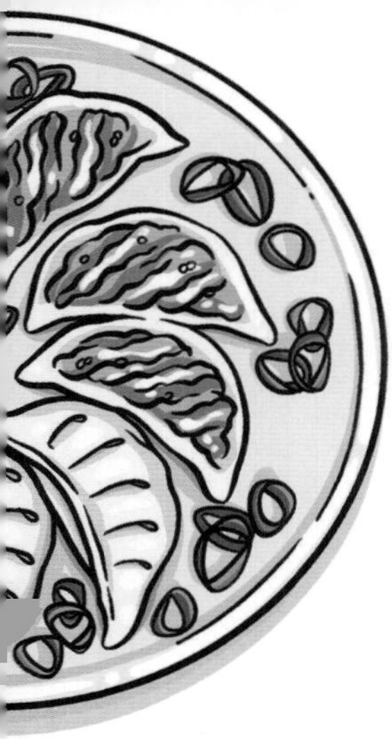

INDEX

B

C

D

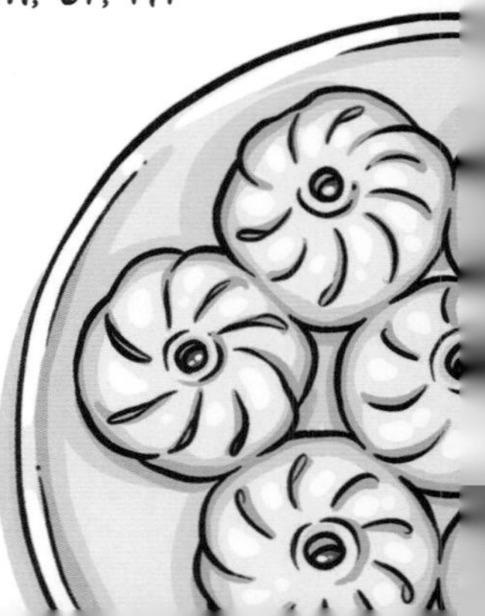

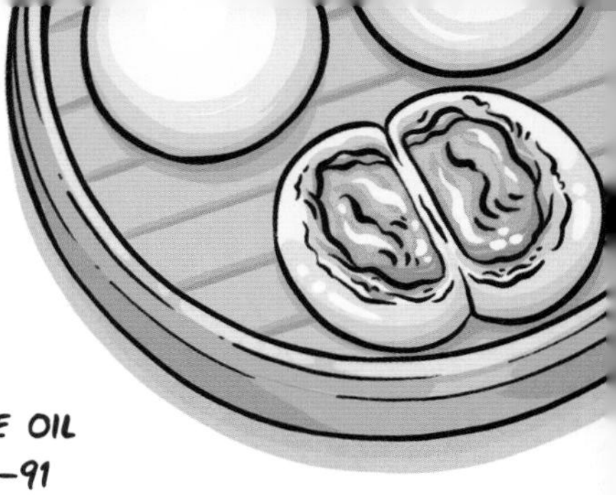

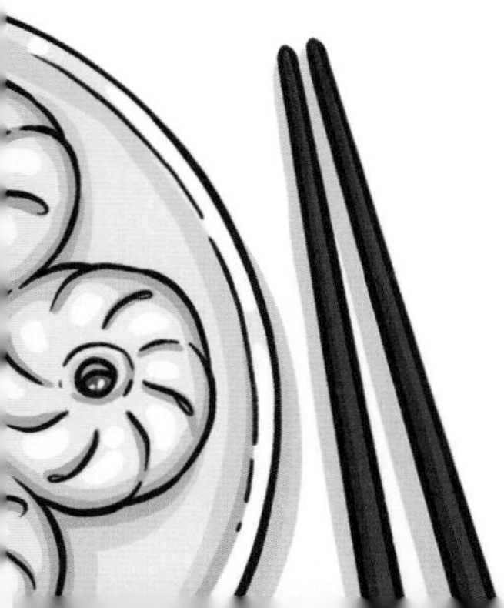

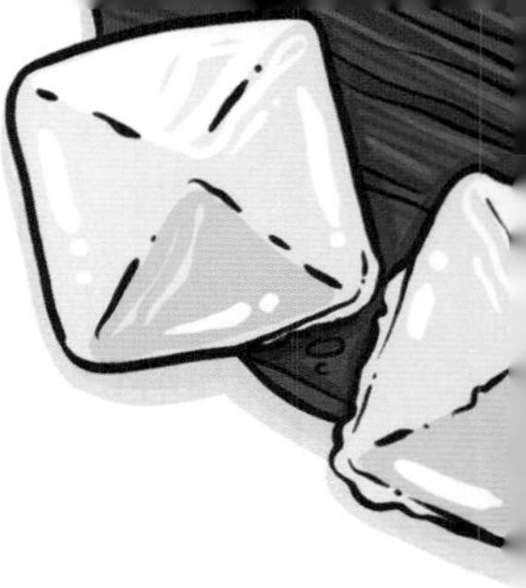

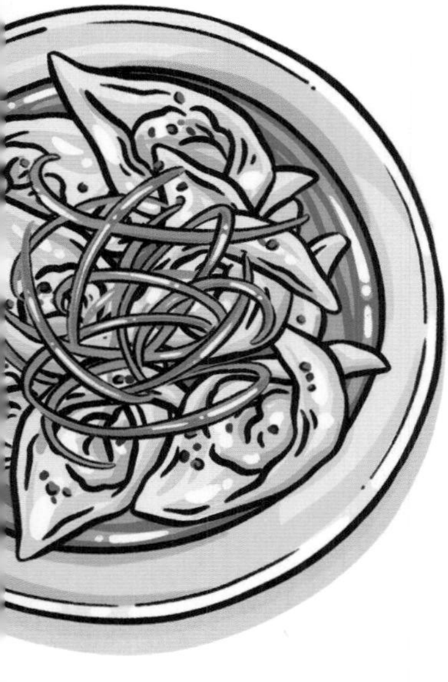

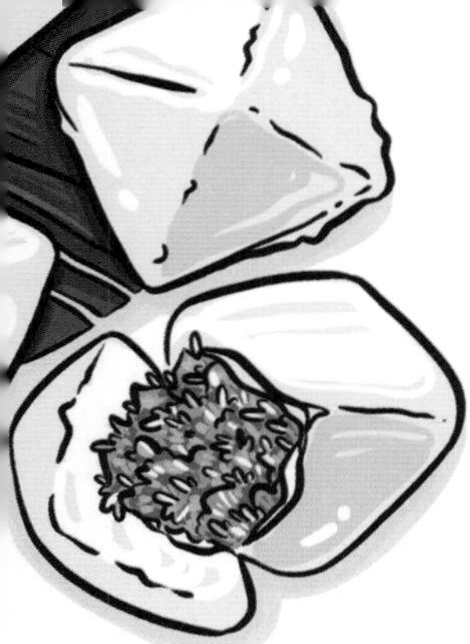

T

W

X

Z

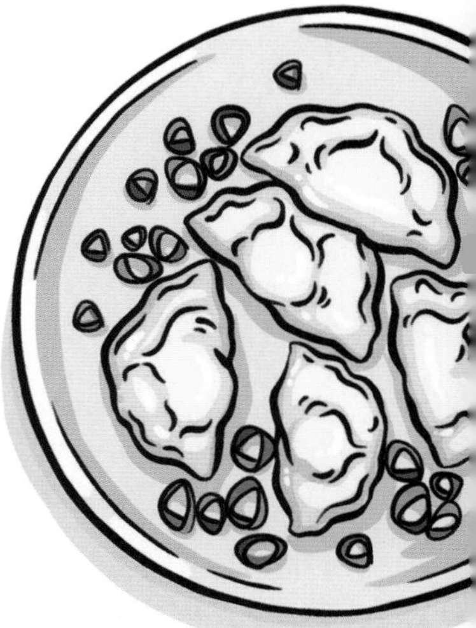

PUBLISHED IN THE UNITED STATES BY TEN SPEED PRESS,
AN IMPRINT OF RANDOM HOUSE, A DIVISION OF
PENGUIN RANDOM HOUSE LLC, NEW YORK.
WWW.TENSPEED.COM

TEN SPEED PRESS AND THE TEN SPEED PRESS COLOPHON ARE
REGISTERED TRADEMARKS OF PENGUIN RANDOM HOUSE LLC.

LIBRARY OF CONGRESS CONTROL NUMBER: 2021931316

TRADE PAPERBACK ISBN: 978-1-9848-5875-7
EBOOK ISBN: 978-1-9848-5876-4

PRINTED IN CHINA

ACQUIRING EDITOR: KIMMY TEJASINDHU
DESIGNER: CHLOE RAWLINS
PRODUCTION MANAGER: DAN MYERS
COPYEDITOR: ANDREA CHESMAN
PROOFREADER: MIKAYLA BUTCHART
INDEXER: KEN DELLAPENTA
PUBLICIST: KRISTIN CASEMORE
MARKETER: ALLISON RENZULLI

10 9 8 7 6 5 4 3 2 1

FIRST EDITION

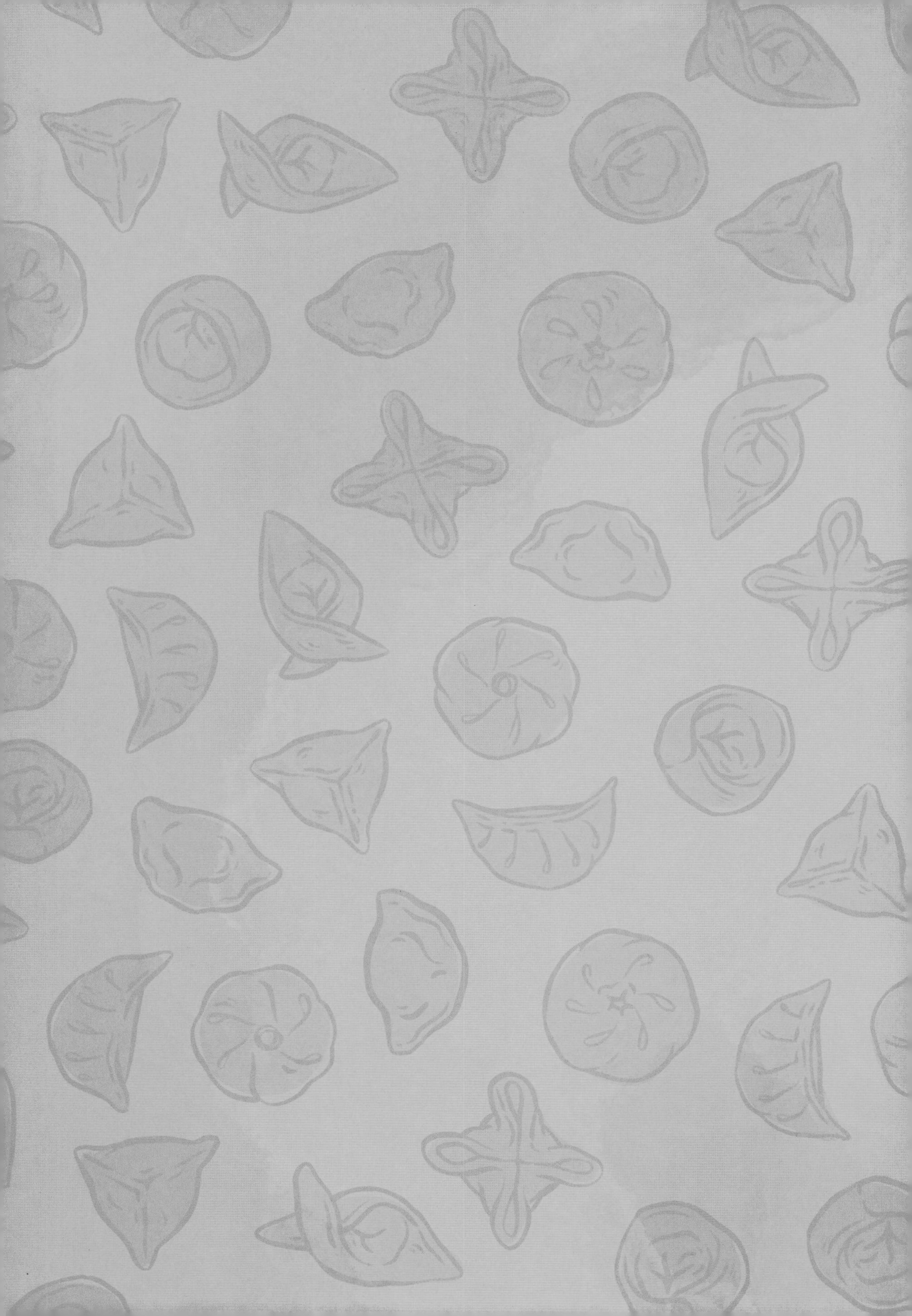

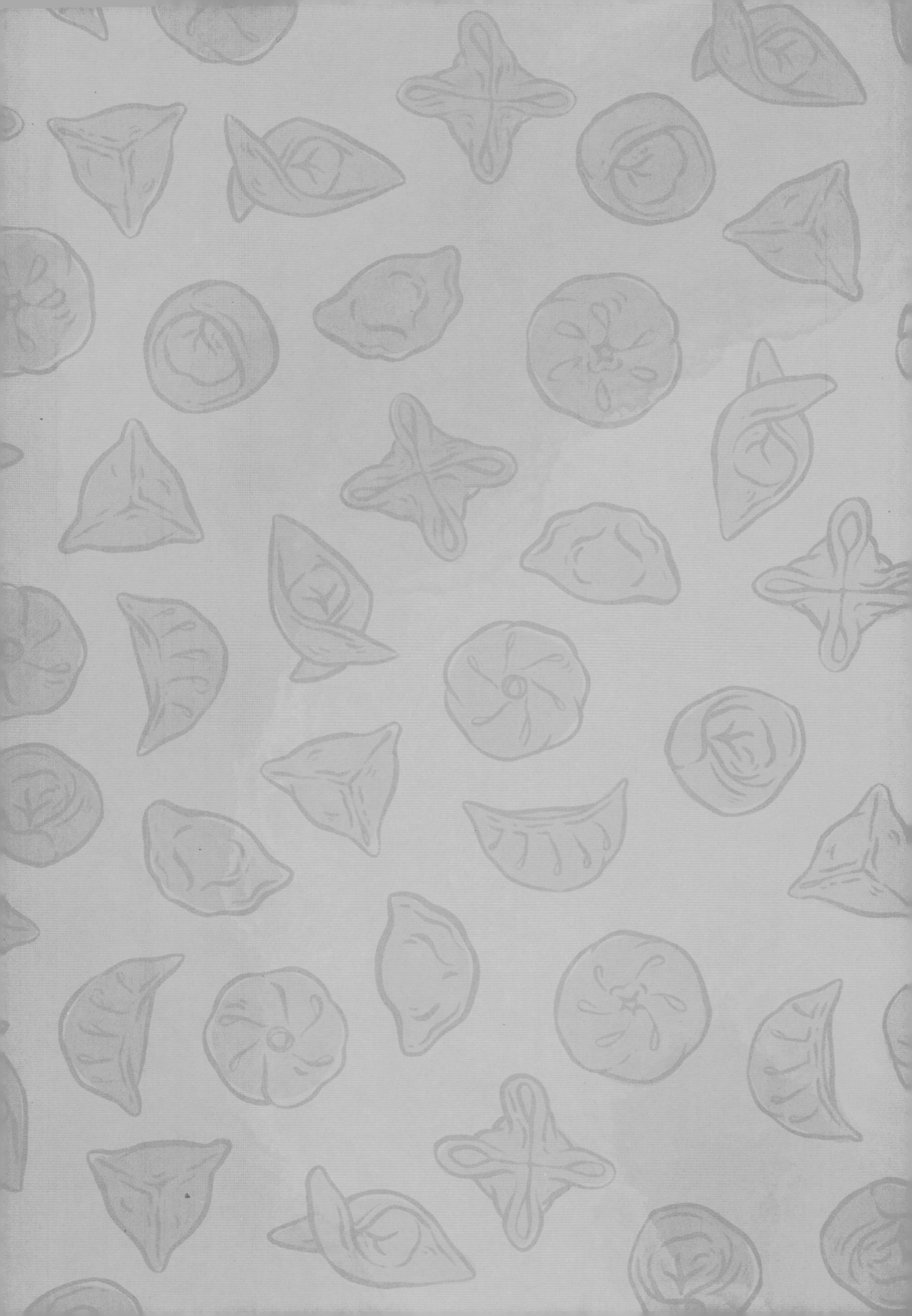